Wireless Security

Wireless Security

Wolfgang Osterhage

Johann Wolfgang von Goethe-University of Frankfurt
Universität des dritten Lebensalters
Frankfurt, Germany

CRC Press
Taylor & Francis Group
an **informa** business
www.crcpress.com

6000 Broken Sound Parkway, NW
Suite 300, Boca Raton, FL 33487
270 Madison Avenue
New York, NY 10016
2 Park Square, Milton Park
Abingdon, Oxon OX14 4RN, UK

Science Publishers
Jersey, British Isles
Enfield, New Hampshire

Published by Science Publishers, an imprint of Edenbridge Ltd
- St. Helier, Jersey, British Channel Islands
- P.O. Box 699, Enfield, NH 03748, USA

E-mail: *info@scipub.net* Website: *www.scipub.net*

Marketed and distributed by:

CRC Press	6000 Broken Sound Parkway, NW Suite 300, Boca Raton, FL 33487
Taylor & Francis Group an **informa** business	270 Madison Avenue New York, NY 10016
www.crcpress.com	2 Park Square, Milton Park Abingdon, Oxon OX14 4RN, UK

Copyright reserved © 2012

ISBN: 978-1-57808-768-6

Library of Congress Cataloging-in-Publication Data
Osterhage, Wolfgang.
  Wireless security / Wolfgang Osterhage.
      p. cm.
  Includes bibliographical references and index.
  ISBN 978-1-57808-768-6 (hardcover)
  1. Wireless communication systems--Security measures. 2. Mobile
communication systems--Security measures. 3. Wireless LANs--Security
measures. I. Title.
  TK5103.2.O82 2011
  621.384--dc23
                                                            2011028410

Printed in the United States of America

Preface

Wireless communication has become popular and pervades many existing newly developed IT applications. In the wake of this development totally new types of security risks have evolved, threatening organizations and individuals and their data and operating environment. This book deals comprehensively with major aspects of wireless security covering most of the communication protocols in use today. It addresses both organizations and private users. To better understand the security challenges the relevant technological background of wireless applications and protocols is laid out and presented in some detail. Special emphasis is placed on the IEEE 802.11x-Standards that have been introduced for WLAN technology. Other technologies covered besides WLAN include: mobile phones, Bluetooth and infrared. This book is based both on personal experience and experience gathered in the course of various security projects in companies. This experience has been condensed into the elaborate checklists provided in the book to guide those responsible for the secure operation of wireless applications. *Wireless Security* is at the same time a guideline and a working tool to implement a security strategy in organizations, assist in documenting the actual security status of existing installations, and helps to avoid pitfalls, when operating in a wireless environment, and in configuring the necessary components.

Niederbachem, Germany
August 2011

Wolfgang Osterhage

Contents

Abbreviations

AAI	Authentication Algorithm Identification
ACL	Asynchronous Connectionless Link
AES	Advanced Encryption Standard
ANSI	American National Standard Institute
ARP	Address Resolution Protocol
ASCII	American Standard Code for Information Exchange
AUC	Authentication Center
BDA	Bluetooth Device Address
BES	BlackBerry Enterprise Server
BSC	Base Station Controller
BSS	Basic Service Set
BTS	Base Transceiver Station
CCK	Complementary Code Keying
CD	Compact Disk
CEPT	Conference Europeenne des Postes et Telecommunicationes
CF	Compact Flash
CRC	Cyclic Redundancy Check
CSMA	Carrier Sense Multiple Access
CSMA/CA	Carrier Sense Multiple Access with Collision Avoidance
CSMA/CD	Carrier Sense Multiple Access with Collision Detection
CTS	Clear To Send
DFS	Dynamic Frequency Selection

DHCP	Dynamic Host Configuration Protocol
DoS	Denial of Service
DSL	Digital Subscriber Line
DSSS	Direct Sequence Spread Spectrum
DUN	Dialup Network Profile
DVD	Digital Versatile Disc
EAP	Extensive Authentication Protocol
EIR	Equipment Identity Register
EMS	Enhanced Message Service
ESS	Extended Service Set
ETSI	European Telecommunications Standardization Institution
EU	European Union
FCC	Federal Communications Commission
FHSS	Frequency Hopping Spread Spectrum
FMC	Fixed Mobile Convergence
FTP	File Transfer Profile
GAP	Generic Access Profile
GFSK	Gaussian Frequency Shift Keying
GHz	Gigahertz
GPRS	General Packet Radio Service
GPS	Global Positioning System
GSM	Global System for Mobile Communications
GUI	General User Interface
HID	Human Interface Device Profile
HIPERLAN	High Performance Radio Local Network
HomeRF	Home Radio Frequency
HR/DSSS	High Rate/Direct Sequence Spread Spectrum
HRL	Home Location Register
HSCSD	High Speed Circuit Switched Data
HSDPA	High Speed Downlink Packet Access
HSP	Head Set Profile

IBSS	Independent BSS
ICV	Integrity Check Value
ID	Identifier
IEEE	Institute of Electrical and Electronic Engineers
IMSI	International Mobile Subscriber Identity
IP	Internet Protocol
ISM	Industrial, Scientific, Medical
ISO	International Organization for Standardization
IT	Information Technology
ITU	International Telecommunications Union
IV	Initialization Vector
Kbit/s	Kilobits per second
kHz	Kilohertz
km	Kilometer
L2CAP	Logical Link Control and Adaptation Protocol
LAN	Local Area Network
LLC	Logical Link Control
m	Meter
MAC	Medium Access Control
MAN	Metropolitan Area Network
MBit/s	Megabits per second
MDS	Mobile Data Service
MHz	Megahertz
MIMO	Multiple Input Multiple Output
MMS	Multimedia Message Service
MPDU	MAC Protocol Data Units
MSC	Mobile Switching Centers
mW	Milliwatt
NAT	Network Address Translation Protocol
OFDM	Orthogonal Frequency Division Multiplexing
OpenSEA	Open Secure Edge Access
OSI	Open Systems Interconnection Model

PC	Personal Computer
PCI	Peripheral Component Interconnect
PCMCIA	Personal Computer Memory Card International Association
PDA	Personal Digital Assistant
PHY	Physical Layer
PIM	Personal Information Manager
PIN	Personal Identification Number
PPPoE	Point to Point Protocol over Ethernet
QAM	Quadrature Amplitude Modulation
RADIUS	Remote Authentication Dial-In User Service
RC4	Rivest Cipher No. 4
RFCOMM	Radio Frequency Communication
RFID	Radio Frequency Identification
RIM	Research In Motion
ROM	Random Access Memory
RSN	Robust Security Network
RTS	Request To Send
S/MIME	Secure/Multipurpose Internet Mail Extensions
SAP	SIM Access Profile
SCO	Synchronous Connection Oriented
SDMA	Spatial Division Multiple Access
SDP	Service Discovery Protocol
SIG	Special Interest Group
SIM	Subscriber Identity Module
SMS	Short Message Service
SPAM	Spiced Pork And Meat
SPIT	SPAM over Internet Telephony
SSID	Service Set Identifier
SSL	Secure Sockets Layer
TCP/IP	Transmission Control Protocol/Internet Protocol
TCS	Telephony Control Protocol Specification

TKIP	Temporal Key Integrity Protocol
TPC	Transmit Power Control
UMA	Unlicensed Mobile Access
UMTS	Universal Mobile Telecommunications System
USB	Universal Serial Bus
VLR	Visitor Location Register
VoIP	Voice over IP
VPN	Virtual Private Network
WAP	Wireless Application Protocol
WECA	Wireless Ethernet Compatibility Alliance
WEP	Wired Equivalent Privacy
Wi-Fi	Wireless Fidelity
WIMAX	Worldwide Interoperability for Microwave Access
WLAN	Wireless Local Area Network
WMAN	Wireless Metropolitan Network
WPA	Wi-Fi Protected Access
WPS	Wireless Provisioning Service
XOR	eXclusive OR

1

Introduction

This book depicts in a condensed form but still comprehensively the actual state of the art of wireless communication technologies. Special emphasis is placed on security aspects. The following subjects are covered:

- WLAN
- PDAs
- mobile phones
- Bluetooth
- infrared

These fields have not been included:

- radiation scattering
- VoIP in detail
- Skype

As WLAN represents the most extensive and basic subject, its chapter is somewhat longer than those for the other technologies, comprising basics, devices and configuration. It is not important to read the complete book, if one is interested in a specific technology like mobile phone security. Each chapter stands alone for itself.

After introducing the technological principles possible risk scenarios will be presented, followed by organizational and technical countermeasures. Both risk scenarios and countermeasures do occasionally overlap between different subject areas or technologies (PDAs and mobile phone for example). Since the book is structured along the lines of technologies and not according to security aspects redundancies are inevitable. This is meant to be so, since each chapter is supposed to speak for itself.

This is also the case for the comprehensive checklists appended to each chapter. They all start with strategic approaches to be followed by more technical details later. The lists are presented in two-column tables. In the left column questions are posed, the right one contains explanations (why is this question of importance?). Once questions are relevant to security aspects regarding serious threats the next line in the table in italics will contain a note having the character of a warning.

For many security problems organisational measures will be proposed. Therefore in some places directives are referred to. The chapters on PDAs and mobile phones contain each simple directives as implementation rules. The final chapter deals with a comprehensive security policy structure, to be imbedded into the general strategic corporate documentation. The introductory passages of the policy can be adopted more or less as presented. For details regarding a specific technology a structure is provided, which can be completed by feeding in content from the preceding chapters.

Although many examples and scenarios have been taken from everyday operations of companies, including solution proposals, the security problems described are equally relevant to the usage of wireless communications by private individuals. Most of the questions in the checklists apply both to a single home station and large computer networks in companies as well. This is also true for the relevant technical countermeasures.

Other practical assistance is given by configuration dialogues for WLAN, PDAs and Bluetooth devices. As an example for a particular type of device BlackBerries are introduced together with its own dedicated security philosophy. Otherwise the state-of-the-art of the technologies in question has been taken into account as far as it has entered the market. In view of the short lividness of technologies this can, however, be only a snapshot, which hopefully will maintain some relevance for some time.

2

WLAN

2.1 WLAN BASIC PRINCIPLES

Interconnections of computers and their components have reached a new level of quality for private users and organizations as well with the deployment of wireless technologies. The development of the WLAN ("Wireless Local Area Network") was a milestone in this process. WLANs bring with them their very specific security requirements, which will be covered in this section.

The following aspects will be covered in detail:

- WLAN general features
- security requirements
- overview of the relevant standards
- ISO layers and encryption,

supplemented by:

- WLAN architectures
- components
- configuring a WLAN,
- application examples and
- a security checklist.

2.1.1 Advantages of Wireless Networks

Making cables obsolete not only saves investing in them, it also offers mobility of a kind previously not experienced by the user. The typical image of a person sitting in the garden at home at work with a notebook illustrates this convincingly. Imagination carries this even further by suggesting this possibility – via notebook,

PDA or Smart Phone – in any place in the world near a hotspot to link up to the company network or the Internet.

2.1.1.1 Mobility and Portability

Besides the changes to working processes already triggered by mobile phones, mobile networks offer an additional push to develop business processes further. This is true for example for large building sites, for the management of sizeable stores, but also for the functioning of medical centers or clinics. Quick access to medical data e.g. can be life saving. Through mobile link-ups work interruptions can be minimized, since the required information is accessible from any given location at any time.

Mobile types of networks permit access to data in real time – just as with a classical LAN. But mobile networks gain in importance, where hard wiring requires high technical expenditure, or special provisions at protected architectural sites for example. In any case the WLAN solution makes even more sense, when setup and operations are only of a temporary kind like at trade fairs or for project teams working together only for a limited period of time. Not only can the cabling be saved, but radio networks can be set up much quicker than classical ones.

WLAN applications have experienced a boom in the private sphere. But since quite often professional experience is lacking there, the security risks are higher.

2.1.1.2 Security

A wireless connection is exposed to other endangerments than fixed networks. The reason lies in the choice of radio itself. An attacker could eavesdrop on an application in someone's home from a nearby car park by using his notebook and a chips can with an antenna.

Such activities are called "wardriving". Meanwhile the Internet offers pages listing unprotected WLANs in certain towns and regions. Therefore there is some urgency to secure radio networking by developing appropriate protective measures.

Wireless access to data in local networks or via the Internet is not critical in terms of security, if the information in question is publicly available in the first place anyhow. However, regarding the exchange of sensitive data, there are additional security challenges with regard to ordinary computer networks. These are due to the specific dangers brought on by the technology itself. Radio waves as carriers of information can be tapped and can be disrupted.

The security provisions offered by the first generations of WLANs soon showed major flaws in practice. The encryption protocols known under WEP offer only weak protection and can be broken relatively easily.

Only in 2004 did the IEEE publish specification 802.11i with a standardized security architecture as a solid basis for reliable WLAN solutions. But even today not all WLAN components on the market do adhere to this standard. Therefore intermediate solutions like WPA play a continuing role.

2.1.2 General Features of Wireless Networks

A radio network offering functionality similar to a LAN is called a Wireless Local Area Network, wireless LAN or WLAN [1]. The naming of the network as "wireless" is somewhat broader than the term "radio net", since this may include also infrared for example.

In practice radio nets are usually coupled to wire bound networks thus complementing the LAN to allow for more mobility for certain users. In case of several LANs coupled together they are also called MANs (Metropolitan Area Networks) [2].

2.1.2.1 Radio Frequencies Available

The spectrum of electromagnetic waves used for communications can be differentiated according to frequency and wavelength. For radio and television broadcasting frequencies between 30 kHz and 300 MHz (long, short and ultra short wavelengths) are used, whereas wireless networks work with shorter waves and thus higher frequencies between 300 MHz and 5 GHz.

In 1985 the Federal Communications Commission (FCC) released the ISM band for general use in North America [3]. ISM stands for "Industrial, Scientific and Medical". Frequencies within this bandwidth can be used free of license. Concerning WLANs the frequency range is between 2.4 and 5 GHz. This decision by the FCC opened the possibility for industry to develop inexpensive components for WLANs.

2.1.3 Standards [5,6,7,8]

Communication within a computer network – cabled or wireless – is impossible unless certain rules are followed. These rules are defined in protocols, which are acknowledged worldwide. For WLANs most of the LAN protocols are relevant. In addition protocols concerning the special features of wireless networks have become necessary. To understand how to configure and run them securely a certain understanding of these standards is required.

Only at the end of the eighties of the last century did the IEEE begin to develop suitable standards. In 1997 the first WLAN standard was published under the number 802.11 [4]. In the years that followed several enhancements and extensions were made public, identified by a special letter at the end of the standard number.

In 1999 the IEEE published two more standards, the 802.11a using frequencies within the 5 GHz range, and the 802.11b. The latter is the standard most widely in use today. This goes for private applications, companies and publicly available hotspots as well. 802.11b allows for gross transmission rates of up to 11 MBits/s, most of which is used up for protocol overheads. 802.11b works within the 2.4 GHz frequency range and uses the HR/DSSS procedure. In 2003 the standard 802.11g was adopted, permitting transmission rates of up to 54 MBits/s within the same frequency range. In 2004 the standard 802.11i finally offered an improved safety architecture. Further details to these standards will follow later in this section.

2.1.3.1 *ISO and 802.11*

The standards of the 802.11 group follow the ISO definitions (Open Systems Interconnection Reference Model) by the ISO

(International Organization for Standardization) [9]. This rather abstract model describes the communication between open and distributed systems on a functional basis along seven layers of protocol built upon each other. Open means that the model is not bound to certain company standards; distributed means a decentralized system environment (Fig. 2.1).

2.1.3.2 PHY

If an application attempts to start a communication between two addresses within a network, all the ISO layers – each with its special assignment – are passed through in sequence. The lowest layer is the physical layer (PHY). The protocols belonging to this layer describe connection setup and connection tear-down between the components in question and the transposition of data into physical signals, being electrical, electromagnetic or optical.

2.1.3.3 Connection Control

Above the physical layer resides the Link Layer called Data Link responsible for handling the connection between the sending and the receiving entity and for the reliability of data transmissions. The relevant protocols are used to organize the transformation of the data into packets. On top of this, the transmission of those packets is monitored using functions that are able to detect and sometimes even correct transmission errors.

The third layer, the network layer, takes over the routing process for all error-free data packets. Then the protocols concerning transport, session, presentation and application follow, all of which will not be discussed here any further.

2.1.3.4 MAC [10]

WLAN specific standards only deal with the two bottom layers. As can be seen from Figure 2.2, the 802 family of standards only deals with the physical layer and part of the link layer. For this purpose the link layer is subdivided into two sub-layers: LLC (Logical Link Control) and MAC (Medium Access Control). LLC is defined

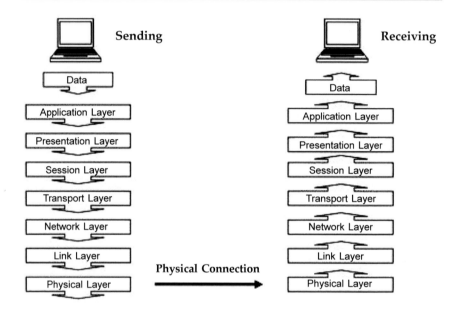

Fig. 2.1 Data Transmission According to the ISO Reference Model

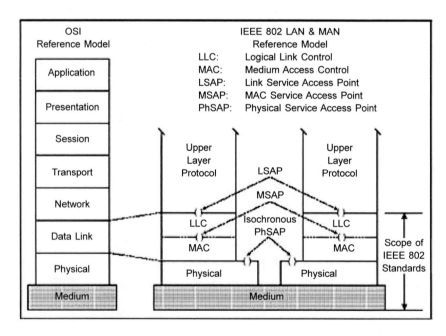

Fig. 2.2 Relationship between the ISO Reference Model and the IEEE 802 LAN/MAN Reference Model (IEEE Std. 802-2001)

in a separate standard 802.2 [11] for all types of local networks. Its protocol manages the connection between sending and receiving computers.

MAC ensures data packaging into so-called MAC protocol data units (MPDU) [12] and controls access to the carrier medium and the mode of operation, which has been defined in the physical layer. The appropriate rules come into play, when several stations share the same carrier medium. The purpose of the MAC protocols is to avoid collisions and in consequence data loss. This could happen, if several stations within the same network try to send and receive data at the same time. To make sure that for a given point in time only one single device is sending, the standard 802.11 uses the CSMA/CA (Carrier Sense Multiple Access with Collision Avoidance) [13] procedure.

2.1.3.5   WLAN as Part of LAN

The advantage of the ISO Reference Model lies in the fact that protocols of the upper layers can access services of the respective layer below and thus do not have to bother about these tasks themselves. A network link thus can be assigned to the link layer to link LANs with different physical characteristics. By contrast routers are assigned to the network layer.

2.1.4   Connecting to Computers

The IEEE 802.11 specification belongs to the LAN/MAN standards all grouped under 802. Initially the standard dealt with components of wireless networks allowing for transmission rates between 1 MBit/s and 2 MBit/s. The envisaged radio technologies included Frequency Hopping Spread Spectrum (FHSS) [14] and Direct Sequence Spread Spectrum (DSSS) [15] as frequency spreading alternatives.

The later versions of 802.11 specified wireless connections with transmission rates of up to 11 resp. 54 MBits/s using different techniques of frequency modulation: High Rate Direct Sequence Spread Spectrum (HR/DSSS) and Orthogonal Frequency Division Multiplexing (OFDM) [16].

2.1.4.1 802.11 and ISM

By adhering to the 802.11 standards the interconnect capability of components from different manufacturers can be guaranteed. At the same time the use of the ISM band has the advantage that it can be used free of license in most countries in the world. This is an advantage especially for private users since no charges come into play, and temporary networks can be put together without bureaucratic barriers.

The problem with the IMS band, however, lies in the fact that it can be used by a number of other technical devices as well. These include medical appliances, microwave ovens, mobile phones and remote control of car ports. Thus WLAN operations could be disrupted by such devices operating close to the frequency ranges in question. So, preventive measures have to be taken.

2.1.5 Antennas

The transmission power of WLAN components depends also on the type of antenna employed. State-of-the-art components have a range between 200 to 300 meters. The achievable range, however, is strongly dependent on various local conditions. Additional antennas enable to bridge longer distances. Directional radio antennas can cover several miles. The increase in range is called antenna gain.

2.1.5.1 Antenna Types and Antenna Gain

Antenna types are classified according to propagation patterns and amplification method. One distinguishes between omnidirectional and unidirectional antennas. The latter have a much longer range, since they operate only at a narrow aperture angle with the same transmission power. This is another form of antenna gain.

Access points usually rely on omnidirectional antennas. Directional antennas are only used to overcome longer distances. Instructions regarding how to build antennas can be found in the Internet. This poses an additional security problem.

2.2 IEEE 802.11 OVERVIEW

Table 2.1 gives an overview about the historical development of the IEEE standards in question:

Table 2.1 Development of 802.11 Versions

Standard	Year	Features	Frequency Range GHz	Transmission Rate MBit/s
802.11	1997	first version, physical layer, FHSS, DSSS	2.4-2.485	1-2
802.11	1999	revision	2.4-2.485	1-2
802.11a	1999	OFDM	2.4-2.485	6, 9, 12, 18, 24, 48, 54
802.11b	1999	HR/DSSS	2.4-2.485	5.5, 11
802.11d	1999	MAC, international harmonization	2.4-2.485	5.5, 11
802.11g	2003	OFDM	2.4-2.485	6, 9, 12, 18, 24, 48, 54
802.11h	2003	MAC, TCP, DFS	5	54
802.11i	2004	WPA	5	54
802.11n	2010	MIMO, channel bonding	2.4, 5	100

The standards of the 802.11 family have been tailored to make wireless communication compatible with Ethernet solutions.

The 1997 Version:

In 1997 the first version of a WLAN standard was released under 802.11. The document outlines the data handling in the wireless context with respect to the ISO physical layer. The specification details the frequency spreading methods—FHSS and DSSS. Originally the standard proposes gross transmission rates of 1 MBit/s for FHSS and 1-2 MBit/s for DSSS.

Communication between any two participants can function either in the so-called ad hoc mode or via base stations (access points). The latter is called infrastructure mode.

When buying a WLAN component the device designation is preceded by a reference to the standard version, for which the device has been released, for example: 802.11b Wireless USB Adapter. The figures relate to the IEEE standard for WLANs, the letter indicates one of the various versions of the standard. These letters again refer to the different Task Forces within the IEEE Work Group for WLAN Standards. Further down the different versions of standard development since 1997 will be outlined.

Since in most countries the 2.5 GHz band can be used license-free and without restrictions, chiefly products using the standard 802.11b are in circulation. More recent products support 802.11g or even 802.11i. This raises the question of compatibility between the various versions. More and more products enter the market supporting several different versions. Netgear, D-Link, Lancom or 3Com offer access points for professional use supporting operational modes for 802.11a, b and g or 802.11b and g or alternatively b or g.

Some notebooks are equipped with integrated WLAN functionality by Intel's Centrino Technology [17], so that a special adapter is not needed. Besides the support for 802.11b a two-band solution 802.11a/b is possible supporting both modes 802.11b/g.

2.2.1   The Standard 802.11 and its Extensions

Note: Here the performance characteristics of the different versions of the standard and their improvements are outlined successively, while going through these versions. The respective security relevant features are detailed in Chapter 5.

The specifications of 802.11 define, how to set up, maintain and tear down a connection within a radio network for the physical layer. For the link layer only the medium access control to the WLAN medium has been defined.

The second partial layer of the ISO link layer (LLC) is not specifically addressed by 802.11. For this the 802.2 standard initially developed for LANs has been adopted. In other words, the MAC layer access protocols have to deliver results compatible to a LAN:

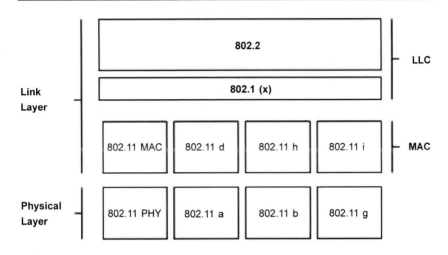

Fig. 2.3 Standard Versions in ISO Layers

2.2.1.1 802.11

The original Standard 802.11 of 1997 defined the modulation methods—FHSS and DSSS—for radio networks with respect to the physical layer. Data transmission rates are limited to gross 1 or 2 MBit/s. The transmission band is 2.4 to 2.485 GHz.

The standard also specifies the operational modes "ad hoc" and "infrastructure". For the MAC layer access rules are defined and the WEP encryption procedure [18] is offered as a possible security mechanism. This basic version of the standard was revised in 1999 superseding the text of 1997. Components corresponding to these basic specifications are only rarely still in use today.

2.2.1.2 802.11a

Already in 1999 the basic specification of 802.11 was enhanced by two new versions: 802.11a and 802.11b. With 802.11a the OFDM procedure was added to the physical layer as a new feature. OFDM allows a much higher data transmission rate and uses a different frequency band. Gross data rates available from then on are: 6, 9, 12, 18, 24, 48 and 54 MBit/s (proprietary extensions by some manufacturers even obtain 108 MBit/s). The stations always try to operate at the maximum possible rate. If they are located close to each other a higher rate is used. If transmission errors occur because of range problems, the transmission rate is reduced.

2.2.1.3 802.11b

The version with letter b, published the same year, still works within the frequency band of 2.4 to 2.4835 GHz, but improves the data rate to about 5.5 or 11 MBit/s gross with the help of the HR/DSSS method, being downwards compatible to DSSS. However, this only yields a net rate of about 50% of the nominal. In 2001 another improvement of the specification followed. With 11 MBit/s the WLAN standard attained about the same transmission rate still widely used today in LANs with around 10 MBit/s. The rate is in any case faster then most Internet connections but still somewhat too slow to transmit audio visual media data.

802.11b is actually still the standard, which is used most widely. This can be attributed in part to the WECA (later called Wi-Fi Alliance) [19], founded in 1999, which has promoted the technology by issuing the Wi-Fi logo. Although the transmission rate (11 MBit/s) is considerably less than with 802.11a this standard has the advantage of a longer range between different buildings or outside. Since the 2.4 GHz frequency band is also used by devices working with Bluetooth or mobile phones interferences are possible.

2.2.1.4 802.11d

This specification adds rules to the MAC layer to enable the world-wide deployment of WLAN components. Adaptations of sending parameters and roaming facilities have been added.

2.2.1.5 802.11g

In June 2003 the IEEE released a new WLAN Standard being downwards compatible with 802.11b and again operating in the frequency band 2.4 to 2.4835 GHz. It uses the OFDM method and allows the same transmission rate as 802.11a with a maximum of 54 MBit/s. The range, however, corresponds to that of the 802.11b.

New 802.11g components thus fit in easily in existing WLANs made up of 802.11b components. However, an 802.11g device then changes into a special compatibility mode, meaning that the effective transmission rate is reduced to 10-15 MBit/s.

2.2.1.6   802.11h

With the specification 802.11h some adjustments have been made to the MAC layer for WLANs in the 5 GHz frequency range to take into account European radio regulations. This standard uses the Transmit Power Control (TCP) procedure to reduce the transmission power as a function of connection quality similar to mobile phones. This procedure had been demanded by ETSI for WLANs under 802.11 [20].

TCP makes sure that the required transmission power between communicating stations or between access points and a station remains within a permitted range. To dynamically adjust the transmission power the stations can request information about the connection route between corresponding stations via special TPC Request Frames.

Dynamic Frequency Selection (DFS) is a technique selecting the best frequency at any given time. The DFS automatically changes the channel, if during the utilization of a specific channel another user or technical device is detected (e.g. a radar unit) also operating within the 5 GHz frequency band. Before occupying a channel a test is made to find out, whether a different system uses the same frequency range. In this way unwanted interference of the WLAN within the 5 GHz can be avoided. 802.11a and 802.11h are otherwise compatible between one another.

2.2.1.7   802.11i

IEEE 802.11i is a new security protocol released in June 2004. It has been developed as an alternative for the encryption procedure WEP, which has been criticized heavily. WEP is not simply substituted by an alternative encryption procedure but by a complex security architecture as its name indicates:

Robust Security Network (RSN). This protocol is relevant for the standards 802.11a/b/g/h. Providers like Lancom and others offer the necessary firmware.

802.11i makes it possible to protect even the ad hoc mode. Besides other encryption procedures it uses the Advanced Encryption Standard (AES) [21] and offers cipher key management using TKIP and a secure encryption method for WLAN access defined by the general network standard IEEE 802.1x based on the Extensive Authentication Protocol (EAP) [22]. This standard is not part of the 802.11 family but belongs to the superior 802 family relevant for networks in general. It describes possible procedures for the authentication and authorization of users and components in local networks mainly based on RADIUS [23] and EAP.

RADIUS (for Remote Authentication Dial-In User Service) is a de facto standard for authentication systems with dial-in connections, requesting user name and password for network access. This information is handed over to a RADIUS server for verification and approval. Communication between RADIUS client and RADIUS server is carried out in encrypted fashion. User data are thus not transmitted in plain text as is done frequently in other log in procedures.

EAP is a general protocol for the authentication of users in a network supporting various authentication methods. It is an extension of PPP [24]. If a WLAN user tries to establish a connection to an access point the user is requested to identify himself, and the corresponding information is transmitted to an authentication server.

Part of 802.11i had been anticipated by the Wi-Fi Alliance under WPA. Therefore the Alliance talks about the new standard as WPA2 [25].

2.2.1.8 *Further Development of 802.11*

The following extensions of the standard are planned or are in progress:

- 802.11n [26]: for a faster WLAN with 108 MBit/s up to 320 MBit/s

- 802.11p [27]: for use in vehicles
- Other improvements concern consolidations of older standards, language and data, support for virtual LANs, roaming, mesh networks, performance, interplay between networks of different standards and questions concerning network management.

2.2.1.9   802.11n

Although 802.11n has not been finalized yet components adhering to the actual state-of-the-art are already on the market. Final approval is planned for the beginning of 2010. Work on it had actually started as far back as 2003 with the 2.0 draft in September 2007. There are still outstanding issues to be attended to like support for individual features. The most recent draft version is that of 10.0 from 15th May, 2009.

802.11n works like everything else in the 2.4 and 5.0 GHz frequency bands. Aim is a transmission rate of 600 MBit/s and a range of up to 300 meters. However, these are theoretical values. A practical rate of 100 MBit/s is more likely. This is due to interactions with multiple types of components within a typical network. Since the new standard is backwards compatible with 802.11a, b and g the rate may be even slower yet.

The standard proposes three major technological features: Multiple Input Multiple Output (MIMO) [28], channel bonding and frame aggregation. In MIMO multiple senders and receivers are managed. Via spatial multiplexing data streams are divided up and then sent in separate streams over the same channel simultaneously. The receiver reassembles these streams using a complex algorithm. Besides this, MIMO focuses the energy of the radio beam into the desired direction of the receiver. By channel bonding, 802.11n systems can patch together two adjacent 20 MHz channels into a single 40 MHz channel thus doubling the transmission rate. By combining individual data frames to larger packets, thus reducing the total number of frames and the associated overheads payload again is increased.

Persistent problems with the standard at the moment are high power usage and security degradation. The latter is due to the fact that intrusion detection scans take twice as long as of now, leaving twice as much time for hackers before interception.

2.2.1.10 Non-Standard Versions

Some manufacturers of components and solutions in a specific field think that the functioning of large standardizing committees like IEEE is too slow. This is the reason why sometimes proprietary extensions are on offer. This is also true for WLANs. For example a version with the designation "802.11b+" has been developed to permit higher transmission rates (from 22 up to 44 MBit/s within the 2.4 GHz band). There are versions for 802.11g with the bundling of two channels and a rate of up to 108 MBit/s. All these are non-official standards concerning the IEEE. And there are possible consequences regarding the compatibility with components of other manufacturers.

2.2.1.11 Alternative Standards

Besides the standardizing projects of the IEEE there have been other efforts to formulate rules for close range wireless data transmission. This was attempted in the first place by the European Telecommunications Standardization Institution (ETSI) having published HIPERLAN/1 [29] already in 1998 and the HIPERLAN/2 specifications in 2000. HIPERLAN stands for High Performance Radio Local Network. The Home Radio Frequency Group published HomeRF [30] for transmission rates of 10 MBit/s in 1998. However, all these alternatives had no significant impact.

2.3   WIRELESS FIDELITY

In 1999 the Wireless Ethernet Compatibility Alliance (WECA) was founded by companies active in the WLAN market. They created the label Wi-Fi (Wireless Fidelity). Later the Alliance was renamed Wi-Fi Alliance. This Grouping wants to make sure that WLAN components correspond to the 802.11 standards.

Such certified WLAN components from different manufacturers can thus be combined as long as they are operated within the same frequency band.

2.3.1 Wi-Fi Protected Access

Because the weaknesses of the 802.11b WEP encryption became known soon the Wi-Fi Alliance had introduced an alternative under Wi-Fi Protected Access (WPA) even before the IEEE itself could release an improved standard. A corresponding certificate was issued for devices adhering to this alternative: Wi-Fi CERTIFIED for WPA. WPA anticipates part of what was later contained in 802.11i in 2004. After 802.11i the Wi-Fi Alliance offers a new certificate: Wi-Fi CERTIFIED for WPA2.

2.4 WMAN

The next generation of WLAN development comprises concepts for radio networks, which can cover longer distances. A special IEEE task force has been created (Task Force 802.16) to deal with Wireless Metropolitan Area Networks (WMAN). These networks will cover areas with a radius of about 50 km with a transmission rate of 70 MBit/s. The frequency range is between 10 and 66 GHz. In 2002 a first draft was issued, followed in 2003 by 802.16. The latter document included frequencies between 2 and 11 GHz. This is the same range used by WLANs. Components on the market today are at present not a serious threat to DSL.

Similar to WLANs with its Wi-Fi Alliance there exists a corresponding interest group to further the proliferation of WMAN – the WIMAX Forum for Worldwide Interoperability for Microwave Access [31].

2.5 KEY TERMINOLOGY

2.5.1 WLAN Components

To build a WLAN one needs certain components, which will be described in more detail later. These components are required to provide an organization or parts of it with a wireless network. On the other hand, they could in turn be used to connect mobile terminals in certain locations to central applications. Or the utilization of a WLAN could be offered to third parties commercially.

As a minimum one needs appropriate network adapters installed on mobile devices. For notebooks one generally uses USB adapters or PCMCIA (Personal Computer Memory Card International Association) cards. The associated drivers assure the necessary send/receive functionality. Recent notebooks have WLAN components already integrated.

2.5.1.1 Access Points

In case the mobile devices do not only want to exchange data between themselves, stationary components are required to serve as an interface to a LAN. These are called Access Points (AP). Quite often these components are integrated into a more general device offering router functions, hubs, DHCP server functionality or a DSL modem. These devices also support the NAT (Network Address Translation) function [32], i.e. the possibility to work with different IP addresses within the same network, but showing externally only a single IP address to the Internet for example. This does not only permit collective access to the Internet, but can also function as a firewall to prevent undesirable access from the Internet to the various stations of the network.

Access point functionality can also be realized by special software on a PC.

2.5.2 Bandwidth

An important role is played by the carrier medium transmission capacity. Any possible data rate depends on the bandwidth, i.e.

the frequency range of the signal transmission. By increasing the bandwidth the amount of information to be transmitted per interval increases as well. Bandwidth is measured in Hertz (Hz) or kHz, MHz, GHz. The rate of data transmission is given in Kbit/s or MBit/s. If a transmission in both directions is possible, this is called a duplex connection otherwise it is a simplex connection. A connection is called half-duplex, if the connection direction can be swapped.

2.5.3 Range

Radio waves are electromagnetic, and they propagate in vacuum with the speed of light. The received power decreases with the square of the distance, which means that the range of transmitters has a principal limit. The realistic distance a radio signal can travel depends also on signal attenuation, also called damping and of course on possible interference. And the range depends of course on the frequency in use. Signals having a low frequency can have a far range even at low intensity. They can also surmount physical barriers such as walls. This is not the case for signals operating at high frequencies between transmitter and receiver.

Contrary to cable connections the transmission medium in a radio network does not have visible bounds, which otherwise could be located easily. At the same time the transmission medium is basically unprotected against unwanted signals coming its way. There is also no guarantee that all stations belonging to a wireless network can hear each other at any moment. There is always the possibility that stations may be hidden momentarily. The propagation of radio waves varies over time and is not necessarily isotropic in space. Figure 2.4 from the 802.11 specification of 1999 visualizes this effect.

Radio communication thus is somewhat less secure and less reliable than cabled connections.

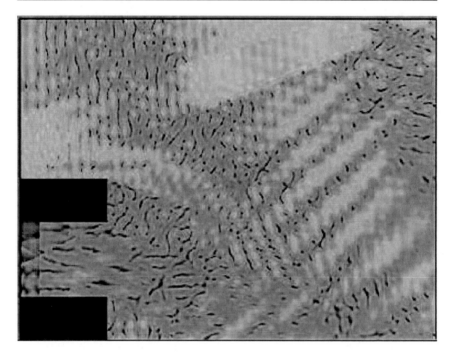

Fig. 2.4   Representative Distribution of the Intensity of Radio Signals (ANSI/IEEE 802.11 1999 Edition)

2.5.4   Channels

As was already pointed out above, WLANs use the frequency range offered by the ISM band [33]. The 2.4 GHz band is divided between 2.4 and 2.4835 GHz into single channels with a width of about 22 MHz each and a gap of 5 MHz between them. Because of spread effects there may be frequency deviations of 12.5 MHz in both directions against the nominal frequency assigned to the proper channel. Therefore interference between adjoining channels is possible.

2.5.5   Channel Separation

Interference can be avoided by using only parallel channels with sufficient separation (Fig. 2.5 and Table 2.2). The best method is to use only every fifth channel, which means that only three channels at maximum can be used in a single WLAN. By reducing interference signals transmission power can be augmented.

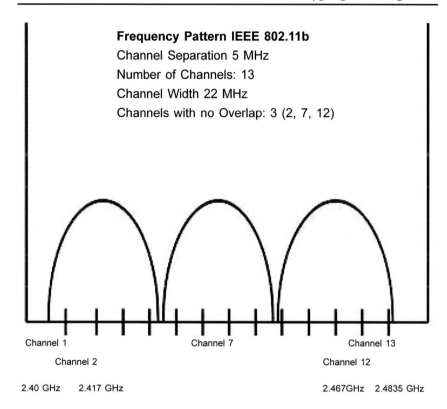

Fig. 2.5 Channel Separation

2.6 ARCHITECTURE AND COMPONENTS

2.6.1 Data Transmission and Synchronization

In its simplest form data transmission in a network functions via a point-to-point connection. Two computers are connected via a carrier medium: cable or radio frequency. Each transmission proceeds in three phases: connection set-up, connection control and connection tear-down. Modems have to synchronize during connection set-up before data can be transmitted. During transmission security mechanisms are active to prevent erroneous transmissions.

Data transmission between sender and receiver is achieved via so-called protocols. They control the data exchange on several layers of communication.

Table 2.2 Frequencies of Different Channels in the 2.4-2.5 Frequency Band

Channel	*Central Frequency [MHz]*	*Frequency Spread [MHz]*
1	2412	2399.5-2424.5
2	2417	2404.5-2429.5
3	2422	2409.5-2434.5
4	2427	2414.5-2439.5
5	2432	2419.5-2444.5
6	2437	2424.5-2449.5
7	2442	2429.5-2454.5
8	2447	2434.5-2459.5
9	2452	2439.5-2464.5
10	2457	2444.5-2469.5
11	2462	2449.5-2474.5
12	2467	2454.5-2479.5
13	2472	2459.5-2484.5

2.6.1.1   *Networks and Routers*

In case more than two participants want to join in the simple point-to-point connection has to be replaced by a network. In order to locate the different participants they have to have addresses.

In large networks several routes between any two stations are possible. Routers can select the optimal path.

If participants want to use the same carrier medium both for sending and receiving, special rules to detect or prevent collisions have to be adhered to. The CSMA (Carrier Sense Multiple Access) pools the most popular ones of these.

2.6.1.2   *Packet Switching*

When telephoning any two participants are provided with a fixed connection during the duration of the call. This is called line switching. The Internet by contrast works by packet switching (Fig. 2.6). The transmitted information is cut up into blocks called packets.

Data Transmission in Packages

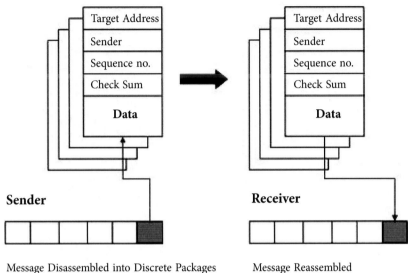

Sender

Receiver

Message Disassembled into Discrete Packages   Message Reassembled

Fig. 2.6 Packet Switching

Every message contains a header with all information required for the data exchange – like the sender and destination address. The packets move autonomously through the net. And it is quite possible that packets – although belonging to the same message and originating from the same sender – will be conducted to their destination via different routes. Only at arrival will they be patched together again.

The advantage of packet exchange is the efficient usage of existing connections, since the data packets are small and they do not have to queue for long. The communication network is available to all participants. All stations can send packets in turn. Errors will be detected immediately. An erroneous packet will be resent. If a station fails the total message will not be lost completely. The packets choose a different route to reach the destination address.

2.6.2 Network Topologies

Networks can be built in quite different ways. The main distinctions are between ring, mesh (Figs. 2.7 and 2.8), star (Fig. 2.9) and bus or tree networks. Radio networks use mesh or star type topologies.

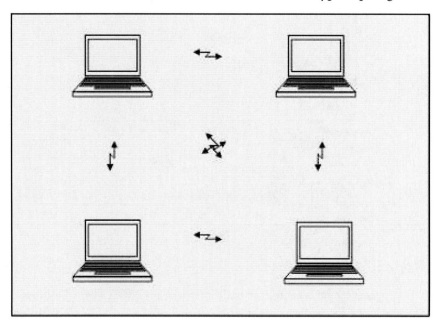

Fig. 2.7 Mesh Network

Those different topologies have certain advantages and disadvantages. In a mesh type network each node may be connected with several other nodes. In a cable network this would lead to rather complex wiring, which can be dispensed of in radio networks. The advantage is higher system stability with no bottlenecks in individual cables. The mesh topology therefore stands for a rather robust technology. It has dominated the total architecture of the Internet, even though the latter is not a pure mesh type network but a mixture of various topologies. Partial mesh networks are alternatives. In partial mesh networks stations are connected to neighboring ones, but not to all others. The minimum configuration of a wireless network is one radio cell with two communicating stations.

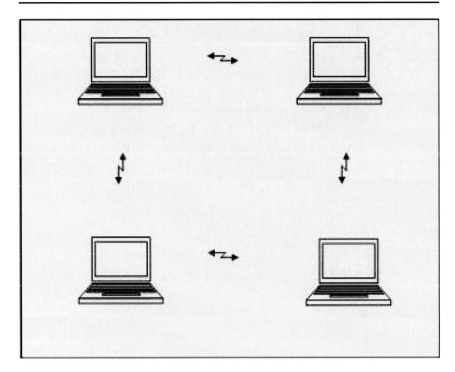

Fig. 2.8 Partial Mesh Network

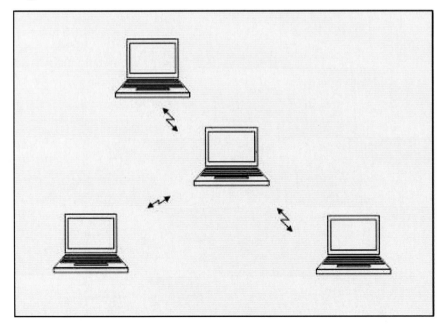

Fig. 2.9 Star Network

In a star type network the individual stations are connected to a central module which can be a server for example by the shortest possible means. In this way the routing is straight forward. The disadvantage is the higher risk of disruption. If the central unit breaks down, the whole network does so at the same time. On the other hand such networks can be managed by system administrators quite easily, since its configuration can be controlled centrally. In a WLAN access points take over the role of the central unit, around which the other stations are grouped.

2.6.3 Special Aspects

While data transmissions via cable are also called "guided" transmissions, radio transmissions are called "unguided". In a LAN each address has a fixed position, whereas in a WLAN an addressed station does not require to have a fixed position.

The data are beamed as modulated radio waves via an antenna from the transmitter and absorbed by the antenna of the receiver. The transmitter transforms its digital bits into corresponding analogue radio signals, which are then detected by the receiver and afterwards retransformed into bit sequences – demodulated.

2.6.3.1 *Modulation and Demodulation*

When modulating a radio wave the signal containing the relevant information is impressed on the fundamental or carrier frequency. The result is a mixed signal. The frequency spectrum of a modulated wave has been changed with respect to the non-modulated one. The type of modulation influences the behavior of the created signal with respect to other signals in the same environment. The stability of the signals depends strongly on the modulation method employed.

A significant step towards better signal stability was the introduction of the spread spectrum method. Its basic idea is to distribute a signal over several channels, i.e. to spread it via modulation with several carrier waves. This makes the signal transmission less sensitive to interference pulses. On top of this less energy is required. On the other hand more bandwidth is used up.

2.6.4 WLAN Architectures

IEEE 802.11 specifies certain structures for the arrangement of components in a radio network. They are called topologies or connection architectures. The spectrum extends from very simple topologies with just a few devices covering a limited amount of space up to complex structures with a multitude of components and theoretically unlimited extension. At a minimum two components are required for a radio network to send and to receive. These components are called stations.

Radio networks generally have a cellular structure, larger networks are subdivided into discrete radio cells. A cell corresponds to the area covered by the range of the radio signals of a particular sender. These ranges again depend on the antennas employed. Such a cell is called Basic Service Set (BSS) [34].

2.6.4.1 Cells and Stations

A BSS can be illustrated as an oval surface, within which all existing stations can reach each other mutually to exchange data

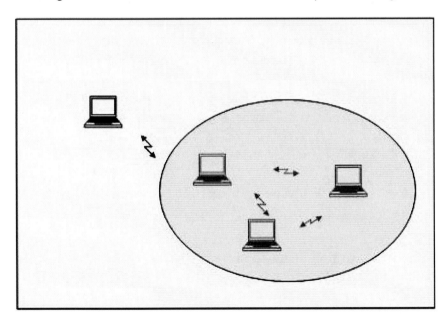

Fig. 2.10 Stations within and without Range

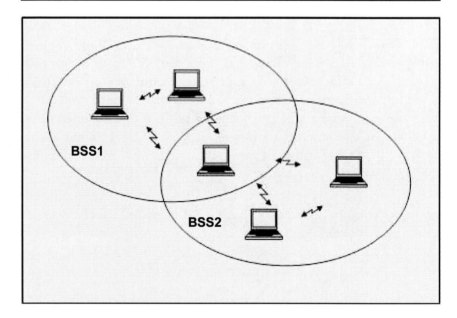

Fig. 2.11 Two Overlapping BSS

(Figs. 2.10 and 2.11). Precondition is that the stations are within reach of each other and operate at the same channel.

If a station is removed far enough such that no other station can reach it any more it is outside the radio cell and therefore outside the BSS.

Radio cells may also partially overlap. In this case certain stations are within the range of all others, but some can only reach part of the stations. They remain invisible to the others. Radio cells can be enlarged simply by adding more stations to them.

2.6.4.2 Ad hoc Networks

In its simplest form a WLAN consists of two computers both equipped with a radio component each to send and receive data (Fig. 2.12). If another notebook gets within reach, i.e. within the radio cell, it can participate in the wireless communication. There is no necessity for hubs as in cable networks.

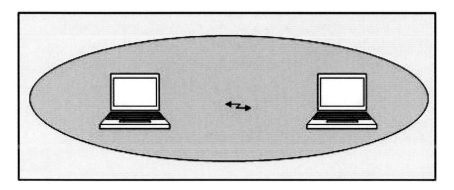

Fig. 2.12 Ad hoc Connection

IBSS

As long as such a radio cell consisting of a few computers can operate on its own this constellation is called Independent Basic Service Set (IBSS). Since there are no elaborate preparations to create such a configuration an IBSS [35] is also called an ad hoc network. Within the ad hoc mode all stations are equal. There are no preferred structures or a center. Data packets are exchanged directly between the individual stations. This type of cooperation is sometimes also called peer to peer workgroup.

In such a WLAN configuration all stations must have activated the ad hoc operating mode, and a common transmission channel has to be set up. The range of such ad hoc networks is limited in buildings to 30 to 50 m. By employing different channels several user groups can constitute separate ad hoc networks not interfering with each other. However, these separate networks cannot get in contact with each other.

Temporary and Spontaneous Connections

The above mode offers itself primarily for spontaneous and temporary networks to organize communication between persons and groups at conferences or fairs, etc. Setting up a network like this is inexpensive since no additional devices are required with the exception of internal and external network adapters. The topology corresponds to a mesh network or a partial mesh network.

Concerning security this type of network, however, is the least secure. In most cases this operating mode does not permit to activate or configure additional security mechanisms. Attackers just have to adjust to the channel utilized to gain access. Only devices corresponding to 802.11i provide for better protection.

2.6.4.3 Infrastructure Networks

The other operational mode for wireless networks is called infrastructure mode (Fig. 2.13). In this case the Basic Service Set is normally integrated into a larger network structure. The individual stations do not communicate directly with each another, but their information is routed via a router called access point.

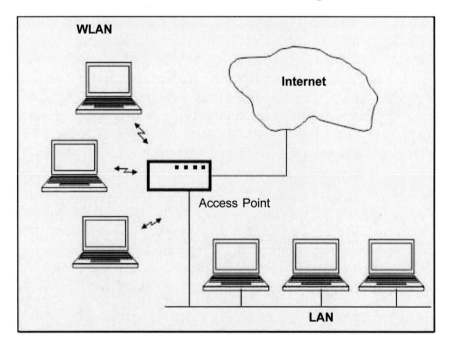

Fig. 2.13 Typical Infrastructure Topology

The access point functions as a central radio bridge enabling communication between the individual stations. An access point is able to serve a radio cell within a radius of between 30 to 150 m. Quite often it not only controls data traffic with client computers acting like a server but also serves as an interface to a cable network.

LAN Portal

Solutions for small businesses or home applications apart - WLANs are deployed mainly as extensions to cable bound LANs. Smooth integration therefore is the general aim and not so much the replacement of LANs by WLANs. However, the emphasis is beginning to shift between the two types of networks with the advent of more powerful and cheaper WLAN components into the direction of WLANs. In many cases, an access point serves as a gateway to the local cable network in a company to provide mobile access to data bases or other resources like printers or scanners. In companies or institutions WLAN solutions are commonly used in combination with classical LAN structures or as extensions. The deployment of WLAN components is especially useful in areas, where high mobility of workplaces is required or where cabling is difficult.

In infrastructure mode one single station within a radio cell takes on a dominant role. In its simplest form a WLAN is a radio cell with one access point and several stations. But there are many more variants possible to realize large scale networks.

Distribution Systems

With the help of access points several station clusters, i.e. several radio cells can be interconnected to a so-called Distribution System (DS). The allocation of the various stations to the BSS however is – contrary to nodes in a wired network – dynamic. Over time stations can move into the range of a specific BSS and then again out of it to a different radio cell.

Two access points can serve as a bridge between two hard wired LANs. Using powerful directional antennas access points can be used to connect buildings somewhat apart but belonging to the same company.

The next stage of expansion is the Extended Service Set (ESS) [36], where several access points communicate to cover a large area of buildings. Once everything has been configured correctly employees with their notebooks can move freely within a building or between buildings. They are passed on from one access point to the next.

Contrary to the spontaneous linkage in ad hoc mode the infrastructure mode makes the creation of a security architecture possible to prevent unauthorized access to data traffic in a WLAN. The adjustments necessary are made during configuration of the access point. These settings determine the rules, which have to be obeyed by stations wanting to participate in a specific radio cell.

Access Points

One single Basic Service Set generally is limited to a circumference of between 30 and 50 m. An intelligent alignment of access points can increase the range of a radio cell to cover distances of up to 100 m (Fig. 2.14). In this set-up the access point acts as the centre of the BSS being surrounded by other stations. All these stations have to be able to reach the access point. However, it is not necessary for all stations to reach each other as is the case for an ad hoc network, because all data traffic is always handled by the access point.

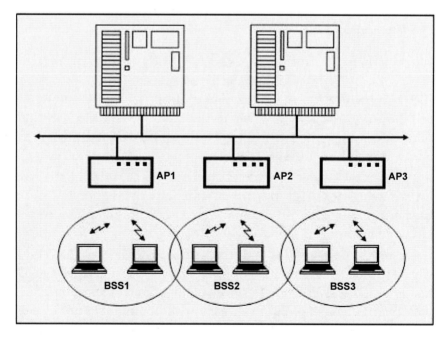

Fig. 2.14 DS with Several Access Points

Bandwidth Distribution

Theoretically one single access point can administrate a maximum 2007 stations. But since the stations belonging to one and the same radio cell have to share the transmission medium, i.e. the bandwidth, the effective maximum number of stations is much smaller. In reality this depends on the data volume to be transferred. Practically quite often 20 stations are a useful limit for a single radio cell, if one wants to work with a transmission rate of 11 MBit/s. If more stations are necessary additional access points have to be installed.

A WLAN operating in infrastructure mode is by definition more complex than an ad hoc mode solution. Therefore almost all the security provisions to be realized for a wireless network refer to infrastructure mode.

If there is more than one access point in a network the task at hand is to make sure that data transfer for the participating stations is maintained without interruption, when these are within the range of several access points. Generally this is assured by the allocation of one single station to only one access point at a given point in time. Once the connection between a station and an access point has been established signals from other access points are ignored. Whenever the station moves close enough to a competing access point and the signal from the first access point is fading a new allocation takes place within the WLAN.

SSID Addressing

Every wireless network is identified by its designation, the SSID [37]. In an infrastructure network all access points belonging logically to that WLAN are endowed with the same SSID. WLAN stations thus can find out by means of the SSID, whether an access point within their range belongs to the WLAN, whom they want to communicate with. On the other hand by allocating different SSIDs an existing WLAN can by subdivided into several distinct networks. This can be useful to separate user groups from one another. All that is necessary is to allocate an appropriate SSID to the stations in question. Stations A, B and C for example communicate via the access point with SSID "WLANone" and Stations D, E and F via access point "WLANtwo".

Each of the stations looks for exactly the WLAN with the corresponding SSID within the tuning range. Once the correct WLAN has been found the connection will be established.

If a station wants to switch between networks, a joker instead of a distinct network designation can be used – normally the designation "Any".

The usage of an SSID has little to do with security since most access points make the chosen name public by broadcasting it. In most cases the administrator can suppress the SSID broadcast by configuring the access point accordingly. This prevents the automatic detection of WLANs around.

When suppressing the SSID broadcast the stations have to know the designation beforehand, if they want to hook up to an access point. But this again is no major obstacle for adequate sniffer tools as long as data are transmitted without encryption.

2.6.4.4   Mobile Internet Access

Current developments have made smaller WLAN solutions also attractive for private applications in households. This is partly owned to the fact that fast DSL connections can be utilized from different locations without having to change any cabling. The necessary WLAN components have to combine with a router or with DSL modems having router functionality integrated (Fig. 2.15).

This solution is preferable to the Internet Connection Sharing (ICS) [38] under Windows XP, because a particular computer does not have to be active to set up an Internet connection.

Access Point as Router

To provide the stations of a radio cell with a common Internet access the access point has to be able to act as a wireless gateway. In this way the access point takes over router and DHCP server functions. For this normally the Network Address Translation Protocol (NAT) is used to hide the WLAN behind a single IP address against the outside world.

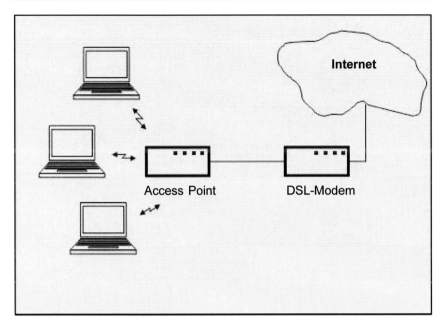

Fig. 2.15 Shared DSL Connection with the Internet

IP Address Allocation

With the help of routing functions data can be transferred from a radio cell to the IP addresses in question to the Internet or vice versa. DHCP takes care of the automatic allocation of the IP addresses for the individual stations within the same radio cell. By employing NAT the IP address for Internet access allocated by the provider is mapped to the individual IP addresses in such a way that several stations can use the Internet access directly even if only one single IP address has been allocated by the provider (Fig. 2.16).

The nice side effect of this is that unauthorized attempts to contact WLAN stations via the Internet are automatically inhibited, because the stations IP addresses are invisible to potential attackers. This solution is comfortable especially for networks belonging to small enterprises or private persons.

Integrating Media Components

Integrating entertainment media like PC, TV or Music have gained in importance. It is possible to direct the output of DVD

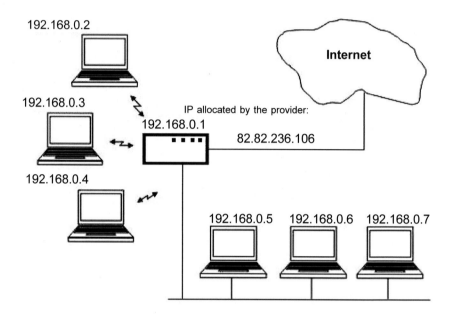

Fig. 2.16 Usage of a Common IP Address with NAT

players to a screen in the living room. The output of Internet radio senders can be routed in wireless fashion to stereo equipment, if the equipment has been fitted with the necessary radio interfaces. These are on offer now in the market.

2.6.4.5 Hotspots

Hotspots are publicly available access points for certain admitted groups. Typical locations for hotspots are airports, railway stations, hotels, fairs, congress centers, cafes and public libraries providing wireless Internet access or other services to be utilized via notebooks, PDAs or smart phones.

Hotspots have been widely accepted by now. The access procedure has to be as simple as possible – charges apart. Generally a GUI is presented to the user, where he can login and the charging process is triggered off, unless the service is free of charge. In most cases access codes are necessary to clear the way into the Internet. These codes are handed out via prepaid cards or voucher.

Hotels offer prepaid cards valid for 24 hrs. The code can only be used once. Codes are also distributed by SMS. Charges are billed to the mobile phone account.

Hot zones are areas, where several hotspots cover them by floating intersections. The open source movement is trying to promote these freely available networks. Such self-organizing networks are on offer in large capital cities, but they are also available more recently between villages in India for example.

2.6.4.6 Open Networks

These community networks are special cases in terms of security, because they are conceived to make available data freely and openly. As long as these networks offer information via established hotspots there is no need for security procedures like encryption or address filtering. To make access as easy as possible a unique designation for an SSID is dispensed of and the joker name "any" is used.

2.6.4.7 Roaming

Roaming is known from mobile telephones networks, especially when travelling abroad. The guest access to a different network happens without notice, but becomes visible through higher charges on the phone bill later.

The term roaming is applied, when mobile users can change without problem from the receiving range of one access point to the receiving range of a different access point in large infrastructure networks. The handover should be completely transparent if possible, especially without interrupting a radio connection to avoid potential data loss during a running transmission.

Roaming is possible through the regular broadcast of beacon frames emitted by an access point to indicate its existence within a radio cell. WLAN stations scan all available channels to locate beacon frames in regular intervals unless they have already been allocated to a specific access point. If a station receives several beacon frames at the same time the signal power decides, which access point will be selected. But as soon as a station separates from access point A and approaches access point B the connection changes without notice by the user and without impact on the currently running data transfer.

Several access points thus can cover a larger area with overlapping radio cells permitting network access anywhere. Users in a big hotel move around from one conference room to the next without loosing their connection to the network. As long as activities take place on the physical layer with separate channels this will work – not excluding the occasional odd problem.

Since the number of possible channels is always limited, a special Spatial Division Multiple Access (SDMA) [39] procedure is available to protect against possible interference. This procedure permits the re-utilization of channels, once radio cells are a certain distance away from each other.

Roaming is of special importance in connection with public hotspots. A single login would provide for movement between different hotspots. Precondition is the harmonization of access procedures.

2.6.5 WLAN Components

One has to differentiate between those components, which are required for a client (adapters) and those required for setting up of the network proper (access points, routers). Adapters can be classified according to the respective clients:

- laptops
- desktops.

Further differentiation depends on the interfaces.

Access points are either singular components or are integrated into a router solution, if more than one network interface is required.

When buying WLAN components certain criteria have to be observed with respect to security and performance:

- number of channels configurable
- configuration of SSID, deactivation of broadcast possibility
- encryption procedure provided
- compatibility with the IEEE 802.1x standard

- possibilities of address filtering
- possibility to use an Access Control List (ACL) [40]
- compatibility of authentication method between access points and clients
- additional mechanisms for access control.

2.6.5.1 Adapters

Adapters for Mobile Terminals

Here we will only consider laptops/notebooks. In the most favorable case the device is already equipped with a WLAN adapter. No extensions are necessary. Otherwise adapters are of the following type:

- WLAN USB adapter
- WLAN cardbus adapter.

WLAN USB Adapter:

This adapter requires only a single piece of cable. It connects with a laptop via a USB plug. The performance of the adapter depends on the throughput limits of the USB interface.

WLAN Cardbus Adapter

A cardbus adapter allows for higher processing rates (Fig. 2.17). The flat card is inserted into the appropriate slot at the laptop. Only the last inch of the card will remain visible displaying two flashlights. Insertion should take place only after the complete boot of the computer.

Fig. 2.17 Wireless Notebook Adapter from LINKSYS

Adapters for Desktops

Adapters for stationary terminals (PCs, desktops), so called PCI adapters, must be fixed into the device (Fig. 2.18). Preconditions are:

- free slot available
- CD-ROM drive
- 500 MHz processor
- 128 MB RAM
- Windows 98 upwards or XP.

Fig. 2.18   Wireless PCI-Adapter from LINKSYS

2.6.5.2   Access Points

WLAN Access Point

This device fulfills all requirements to set up a simple WLAN with clients configured appropriately. Apart from this an Access Point does not offer any other functions like Internet access for example.

WLAN Router

Just like classical routers a WLAN router manages the control of multiple incoming and outgoing signals using parallel channels

Fig. 2.19 Wireless Router from D-Link

(Fig. 2.19). So Internet and WLAN interfaces can be handled at the same time – even an additional telephone switch, Fax, printers, a classical LAN and of course a PC or a laptop as clients. A router is equipped with an antenna, which can be adjusted manually.

2.6.6 Configuring a WLAN

Before configuring a WLAN certain criteria have to be taken into account at the planning stage:

- decision about the authentication method
- shielding against other technical devices emitting electromagnetic waves
- preparing a layout that avoid radio dead spots
- avoidance of channel overlap by multiple users.

The configuring of a WLAN and its components proceeds in three distinct phases:

- drivers
- hardware
- configuration proper.

Configuration procedures differ depending on whether the object is just a simple adapter or a complete infrastructure network. Within the network routers and clients have also to be setup. In all cases detailed instructions for installation – normally on a CD – are usually provided by the manufacturer guiding the user through his options. At this point we will not repeat the user guidance in detail.

2.6.6.1 Drivers

For all adapters driver installation is necessary. The drivers are provided with the adapter on a CD or can be downloaded from the Internet. After loading the usual graphic user prompting takes place. This and all other installations should proceed under the administrator account. In this way the driver will be saved securely on a path decided on by the administrator. This is the only substantial decision required. After finishing the installation the computer has to be rebooted.

2.6.6.2 Hardware and Configuration

WLAN USB Adapter

This is how to proceed:

- insertion of setup CD and start.
- connecting USB plug of the adapter to a USB port available.

After this the user is asked to select an "available wireless network" by means of a choice menu presenting all SSIDs currently available. The user selects the network, with which he wants to work and establishes the connection via "connect". If the target network is not in the list, it can be added.

If the network is to be protected by WEP, the WEP key belonging to the network is requested. Only after entering this key a connection to the network is possible. If protection is controlled by WAP a special passphrase for the net is required as input.

WLAN Cardbus Adapter

This is how to proceed:

- insertion of setup CD and start

- introducing the adapter into the cardbus slot
- start installation

After this the user is asked to select an "available wireless network" by means of a choice menu presenting all SSIDs currently available. The user selects the network, with which he wants to work and establishes the connection via "connect". If the target network is not in the list, it can be added.

If the network is to be protected by WEP, the WEP key belonging to the network is requested. Only after entering this key a connection to the network is possible. If protection is controlled by WAP a special passphrase for the net is required as input.

PCI Adapter

This is how to proceed:

- insertion of setup CD and start.

After positive confirmation and execution of the following steps the computer shuts down. Now the manual assembly of the adapter can start.

The PC encasing has to be opened to find a free slot on the motherboard. The adapter is placed on the PCI slot and its ear fixed with a screw to the PC frame. After this the housing is closed and the antenna attached to the adapter. Now the computer can reboot.

After this the user is asked to select an "available wireless network" by means of a choice menu presenting all SSIDs currently available. The user selects the network, with which he wants to work and establishes the connection via "connect". If the target network is not in the list, it can be added.

If the network is to be protected by WEP, the WEP key belonging to the network is requested. Only after entering this key a connection to the network is possible. If protection is controlled by WAP a special passphrase for the net is required as input.

Access Point

Initially all default settings by the manufacturer have to be replaced by individual security settings to prevent unauthorized access.

Connection of an access point proceeds either directly to a PC by a cross over cable or via a switch or hub in a hardwired network. Switch on access point and start installation CD. The setup assistant searches the net for the access point. Depending on the manufactured type either a new SSID or an automatic assignment of an IP address are possible.

Router

Precondition: modem or DSL with corresponding telephone connection.

Preparation:

- connect power supply
- connect one of the five output sockets of the router via a patch cable to the computer
- connect WLAN interface of the router to the modem.

This is the usual process under Windows ©:

Select "System Control" via the start menu of the computer, select "network connections", then "LAN connection". In the following menu select "Internet protocol (TCP/IP) and properties". Only one single IP address can be obtained automatically or entered by choice.

From now on (for some providers right from the outset) user prompting continues via the Internet browser in the manufacturer's domain. Normally the included IP address has to be entered. The following parameters have to be adjusted:

- router password
- Internet connection type (DHCP, static IP, PPPoE)
- network mode
- SSID designation
- radio channel
- WEP or WAP securities.

2.7 SECURITY REQUIREMENTS

The peculiarities of radio transmissions require special measures to secure wireless communication in local networks. Before detailed procedures from relevant standards are presented a brief summary about the objectives is given:

2.7.1 Assuring Availability

The sensitivity of wireless connections against interference is a general problem. If other technical devices transmit within the same frequency spectrum as WLAN components, WLAN communication will be disturbed or even prevented. These other devices can be microwave ovens, surveillance cameras or Bluetooth traffic. It is also quite possible that an attacker tries to deliberately interfere with WLAN transmissions.

One of the reasons for careful planning and implementing a communications network is to achieve maximum availability. One aspect is the optimal placement of components fixed in locations, i.e. Access Points. Another important variable is the selection of the most favorable operational modus and with this the decision about possible frequency ranges and transmission rates. Because of the sensitive nature of the network constant observation of its performance is necessary to identify the causes for any malfunctioning.

2.7.2 Assuring Data Integrity

In any network – be it wireless or cabled – data have to reach their destination complete and unaltered. Once data have been manipulated on their route, the receiver has to be enabled to detect this fact to be able to react. The effect is the same, whether the manipulation has been done on purpose or whether it was only the result of a transmission error.

2.7.3 Assuring Authenticity

Both sender and receiver of messages have an interest that the authenticity of the other side is guaranteed. Special access controls have to make sure that sender X cannot pose for sender Y. The same goes for the receiver. This is most important for legally binding transactions including commercial orders, invoices, etc.

2.7.4   Assuring Confidentiality

In contrast to communication in public networks, in which publicly available information is offered to anyone, who wants it, confidentiality plays an important role in private wireless networks with respect to data protection. The desired levels of confidentiality have to be implemented in practice. Since radio signals can be listened into the only solution is encryption. Encryption has two objectives:

- to protect transmitted information and
- to protect link data.

2.7.5   Security Risks

The fact that – so to speak – wireless transmissions use free space as transmission medium makes it easier to eavesdrop to them than to data transmitted via cabled connections. The security requirements therefore are different with respect to LANs [41]. On top of that LANs are locally fixed with known users. WLANs neither have visible geographic boundaries nor is it apparent, who is currently connected.

These are the most important motives for attackers and their most common forms of attack:

- Technical challenge: playful Hackers just wanting to find out, whether they can get access somewhere without any intention to wrack havoc; this may include the intention to listen in without the knowledge of other people and to penetrate their private spheres. Tools can be obtained via the Internet.
- Criminal intention: the purpose is to damage other persons or organizations or to enrich oneself.
- Unauthorized sharing of Internet access: if a WLAN is operated in combination with DSL access, someone could try to use the Internet access without authorization. There exists the possibility to misuse some ones account for downloads of confidential data or for criminal contacts.
- To gain direct material advantage: all kinds of unauthorized accesses are imaginable without knowledge by the party concerned even over a prolonged period of time.

- Insertion of data and software via an unauthorized station in a WLAN to drop off selected data. This is done by pretending authorized identity to an Access Point. Examples: implantation of spyware [42], spying data of credit cards, attacks by Trojan Horses [43] to steal important company data; viruses to destroy data.

2.7.5.1 Spying

This is the prime motive for penetrating unprotected WLANs. WLANs are easy to detect, since they broadcast beacon frames into the surrounding space to attract attention. An attacker on the street in his car can collect these frames via an antenna and will gratefully enter this WLAN community as a blind passenger. It is sufficient that he approaches the building in question close enough with his notebook or PDA without being noticed in the first place. With tools anywhere obtainable the WLAN check is done and the names of the Access Points identified. Sniffers [44] can thus enter the range of a radio cell without being detected, collect all data traffic and analyze it.

With special tools the number of WLAN users can be determined and whether the network has any protection at all. Estimates say that the majority of WLANs in operation today is not sufficiently protected. In many cases an intruder can enter a radio cell unchecked.

2.7.5.2 Decoding

Even if a WLAN employs encryption techniques this may not suffice to prevent illegal recording of data. Once the attacker has registered enough data packets he can try to break the cipher key with statistical methods. To break a WEP key e.g. data recording of only a few hours usually suffices. There are tools available to this end in the Internet, which have been developed for the first generation of WLAN components, where encryption mechanisms have been weak. Companies could use such tools themselves to discover weak points in their own WLAN configuration.

WLAN protection at a certain level quite often is not adequate against determined attackers. Even after initial failure more powerful tools will be fielded to arrive at the intended end. Early discovery and continuous observation are therefore necessary.

An additional danger is posed, if an attacker tries to pretend a legitimate user identity with the help of network addresses used in the WLAN and thus obtain access to protected data areas.

The fact that WLANs are prone to spying in one or another way calls for appropriate countermeasures. Part of the strategy can be a WLAN trap to find out, whether attacks from outside are attempted. The euphemism for this is "honey pot network" [45]. Companies can configure a less protected part in their otherwise well shielded network using dummy data for fictional business traffic. By analyzing log files of the Access Point illegal attempts can be filtered out.

2.7.6   Physical Layer

The problem to be solved on this layer concerns the fact that within the frequency range provided many stations may want to transfer data at the same time. This happens, when the range of potential senders and receivers overlap.

2.7.6.1   Spread Spectrum

To be able to distinguish between the different participants FHSS and DSSS are employed to generate the necessary signals. FHSS is the older method, whereas DSSS is used more widely today. Both procedures are not compatible. This means that within a WLAN all components have to follow either one or the other.

The spread spectrum procedures are less sensitive to interference or electronic disturbances than single channel methods.

FHSS

The Frequency Hopping Spread Spectrum was originally developed during the Second World War to control torpedoes. As indicated by its name the radio signal is subdivided into small segments and hops within fractions of a second several times from one frequency to another (Fig. 2.20). The quasi random selection of the frequencies is achieved by the Gaussian Frequency Shift Keying (GFSK) [46] method. To be able to handle the signals the receiver has to know the pattern of these hops.

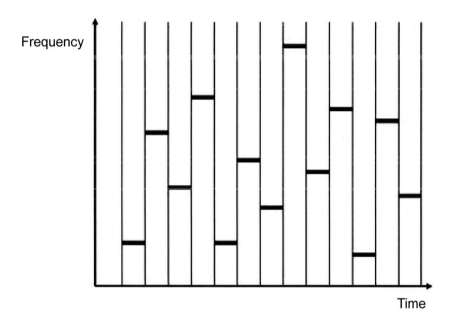

Fig. 2.20 Frequency Hops

Other sender/receiver pairs may at the same time use a different hopping, so that several data transmissions can run at the same time without interfering each other.

If in the unlikely case that a collision takes place, the system sends the data packet again, until the receiver sends a hand shake back. The 2.4 GHz band for WLANs is subdivided into 75 subchannels with a width of 1 MHz each. The disadvantage of FHSS is the relatively high overhead with respect to the useful data generated by the frequency hops. Therefore data transmission with FHSS is relatively slow. The maximum is 1 MBit/s.

DSSS

The Direct Sequence Spread Spectrum procedure is widely used and works differently from FHSS (Fig. 2.21). DSSS uses just one single

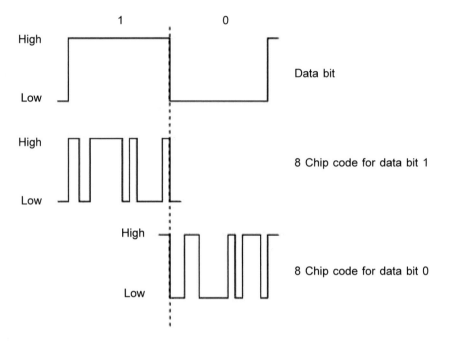

Fig. 2.21 The DSSS Procedure

22 MHz wide channel without frequency hopping. The data stream is combined via an XOR operation with a so-called chip or chipping code. The data is represented by a random sequence of bits known only to sender and receiver. The zero is represented by inverted chipping code.

The code spreads the transmitted data over the available bandwidth. Longer chips need a wider bandwidth, but increase the probability that the data are transmitted correctly.

The advantage of DSSS is that the receiver can easily find out, whether the data have originated from the same sender that has generated the code. The procedure also facilitates error checking, since bit patterns not corresponding to the code can be filtered out. If there are one or two bits in the pattern, which have not been transmitted correctly, an automated correction takes place without having to send the data again. Since the protocol overhead is less than that for FHSS higher transfer rates are possible. Newer variants of 802.11 take that into account.

With DSSS the data packets are extended by a 144-bit prefix. 128 bits are used for synchronization and 16 bits for a start of frame field. This is followed by a 48-bit header with information about the transmission rate, the length of information within a packet and a control code. Since only the header fixes the transmission rate of the succeeding user data, the header itself is always transmitted with 1 MBit/s beforehand.

Even though the prefix will be removed in the further process its length is still taken into account, when calculating the transmission rate. The effective transmission rate thus is always less than the nominal rate.

HR/DSSS

An improved option of DSSS is called High Rate Direct Sequence Spread Spectrum (HR/DSSS). This is the frequency spreading procedure most commonly used in WLANs. Just as DSSS itself HR/DSSS operates within the 2.4 GHz band. It uses a modulation technique called Complementary Code Keying (CCK) [47]. Data can be transmitted at a rate of up to 5.5 or 11 MBit/s.

OFDM

Another option for signal generation in radio networks is called Orthogonal Frequency Division Multiplexing (OFDM). This technique operates within the 5 GHz band. Contrary to FHSS and DSSS OFDM transforms the digital data into multiple analogue signals in parallel. The frequency bands are separated into four channels each, which are split again into another 52 subchannels of 300 KHz width each. The subchannels may overlap. Interference is avoided by scheduling. The advantage of this procedure is a much higher transmission rate.

The transmission rate depends on the modulation technique employed. With Binary Phase Shift Keying Modulation (BPSK) [48] 6-9 MBit/s can be obtained, with Quadrature Phase Shift Keying (QPSK) 12-18 MBit/s and with Quadrature Amplitude Modulation (QAM) 24-36 MBit/s.

Furthermore OFDM was applied to the 2.4 GHz frequency band with the aim to obtain similar transmission rates here as well.

2.7.7 Medium Access Layer

The procedures specified by WLAN standards for accessing the transmission medium generally differ from those in the 802 family defining accesses in local area networks. These differences are due to the nature of wireless transmissions. The 802.11 standard defines different services for the carrier access layer controlling data exchange within the network. These services concern the way, in which data are prepared for transmission and the necessary security provisions.

2.7.7.1 Frames and Fragmentation

If data are to be exchanged via a wireless connection, they have to be divided up and packaged in a suitable way. The 802.11 standard calls these MAC protocol data units (MPDUs) [49]. It defines exactly how such a data packet or frame should look like. There are different types of frames: data frames for user data, control frames for control data and management frames to manage the network operations.

A data frame consists of a MAC header, the frame body containing the user data and a frame check sequence, containing a check sum as a 32-bit cyclic redundancy check (CRC) [50]. Figure 2.22 shows the components of a data frame.

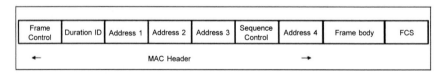

Fig. 2.22 Components of a Data Frame

Whereas the length of the frame body can vary, all other fields and their sequence are fixed. The first address contains the target address of the final destination, the second address is the original address of the sending station, and the remaining addresses control the forwarding.

When configuring an access point a fragmentation threshold can be defined. This value determines the maximum packet length. If this length is exceeded the packet is divided up into so many more fragments.

2.7.7.2 Avoidance of Collisions

The MAC layer controls primarily the data traffic within the radio network. 802.11 defines several methods for that purpose. One aspect is the avoidance of collisions. Collisions would otherwise occur, when several stations are sending data packets at the same time.

CSMA/CA

The access to a radio channel in systems according to the 802.11 standard is controlled by a random procedure called Carrier Sense Multiple Access with Collision Avoidance (CSMA/CA) [51]. This technique permits the simultaneous access of several devices to the carrier medium. The working of CSMA/CA can be described in the following way:

When a station wants to send a data packet it checks the carrier medium, whether other signals are present. If it cannot detect any signal it waits for a short random time interval (inter-frame spacing) and then checks again, if the medium is clean. If this is the case the data packet is transmitted. The station having received the packet checks its integrity. If everything is OK, a receipt is sent after another short inter-frame spacing. If the sending station does not receive an acknowledgement, it is assumed that a collision with a different data packet has taken place. The station waits again for a random time interval and then tries again.

RTS/CTS

An optional extension of CSMA/CA is RTS/CTS [52]. This procedure is applied to master the problem of "hidden" terminal devices. These are devices, which sometimes cannot be reached because of signal attenuation. Initially the station which wants to communicate transmits a "request to send" a packet to reserve a transmission channel. The receiver acknowledges this with a "clear to send" packet. All other stations remember the holding time established by the RTS/CTS packets and refrain from sending data themselves during this time interval. If more than one station tries to send data at the same time, CSMA/CA instructs all other stations safe one to refrain and try again later.

While configuring an access point one can normally define a threshold. This value determines, whether the packet transmission can be handled by the CSMA/CA or by the CSMA/CD [53] method otherwise used in LANs as a function of packet size. In the latter case the packet will be sent after a certain holding period.

2.7.7.3   MAC Addresses

The protocols of the 802.11 MAC layer operate within the same address space generally provided for local networks adhering to the 802 standards family. To identify components the Medium Access Control (MAC) address is used. This is a unique 48-bit serial number assigned by the manufacturer of the relevant network component. The first 24 bits contain the manufacturers ID, assigned by the IEEE, the rest is filled up by the manufacturer himself. This number is generally represented in hexadecimal code like 00-09-5b-e7-b3-5c with a hyphen as separator (Fig. 2.23).

#	IP Address	Device Designation	MAC Address
1	192.168.0.3	MYTRAVELMATEXP	00:00:e2:30:6e:82
2	192.168.0.4	DELLPROF	00:10:5a:bb:0b:cb
3	192.168.0.5	FUJI	00:30:f1:15:4b:6f

Fig. 2.23 Device List in an Access Point with the Mapping for IP Addresses to MAC Addresses

MAC Addresses and IP Addresses

With the help of MAC addresses the MAC layer can get in touch with higher levels of the ISO model. In this way it is possible to assign for example an IP address to a component with a specific MAC address. This mapping is done by the Address Resolution Protocol (ARP) [54].

Since both LANs and WLANs use MAC addresses in the same way it is no longer possible to distinguish, whether a user utilizes a LAN or a WLAN component at the Internet protocol level.

Address Filtering

Access points have the option to have special MAC address filters configured, so that only stations with defined MAC addresses will have access, which is denied to others. For this purpose tables have to be manually administrated, which can be tedious in large networks. On the other hand one of the known security problems is the fact that MAC addresses can be faked. When an attacker finds a registered MAC address, he can program his own device to show just this address to the network. This is called MAC address spoofing [55].

2.7.7.4 SSID Network Name

Each wireless network can be identified by a network designation. This name can be chosen arbitrarily and is called the Service Set Identifier (SSID). Its length can be up to 32 characters. This value can also be set to "0" (zero) corresponding to operation mode "any". In this case any station can hook up to the access point. The access point broadcasts this mode at regular intervals as beacon frames to attract attention. In case it has a proper designation, however, the access point waits for the polling of stations, to which the SSID is known.

In this way the SSID can be used to control access. But this mechanism is of limited value, because the SSID designation is transmitted unscrambled and can thus be easily detected. This is particularly precarious once the designation allows for conclusions as to the name of the user or his company. This is to be avoided.

2.7.7.5 Authentication Procedures

It has already been mentioned that the nature of wireless networks and their mode of connection makes them particularly prone to data theft and spying. To impede this several authentication methods have been defined on the MAC layer. Before a station can communicate with a WLAN, authentication has to take place to verify the identity of the station as being a registered member of a group of stations constituting the network. There are two types of authentication: Open System and Shared Key.

Open System [56]

This first type being the default basically dispenses with a proper authentication and is therefore called "null authentication". Every station requesting an authentication of this type gets it from every other station configured in the same way. The procedure works in two stages. At first the authentication is requested and thereafter confirmed, if it works out to be correct. Only thereafter communication within the WLAN is granted. As long as all the components within the network operate with open system authentication, any notebook can share messages with all reachable networks as long as they are not encrypted.

Shared Key

The Shared Key authentication can only be applied, when the Wired Equivalent Privacy (WEP) mechanism is activated. This procedure requires that the station and the access point own the same key. The station has to prove to the access point that it knows the key indeed. This happens by sending a test piece. This operation proceeds along the following line:

The sending station emits an authentication request to the access point. It includes its own MAC address to identify itself and an Authentication Algorithm Identification (AAI), which controls the authentication method – in this case a "1" for Shared Key and a sequential number, controlling the sequence of the four authentication steps.

The access point replies with the same AAI, adds first a 1 to the sequential number and then a random number of 128 bytes in length.

In its turn the station encrypts all three elements with a shared key, while increasing the sequential number and returning everything to the access point.

The access point checks the reply and decrypts the test message. If it matches this is proof that both cipher keys correspond. The access point sends an acknowledgement to the station and permits access to the network.

This procedure allows a well directed message exchange within a specified sample of participants.

Wired Equivalent Privacy (WEP)

From the beginning the standard IEEE 802.11 provided for security architectures to deal with the sensitivity of wireless connections. WEP offers a basically symmetrical encryption procedure to deny unauthorized access to sensitive data by trespassers. The secret cipher key is simply distributed between access point and adjacent stations. How this should happen is left open by the standard. This means that within one and the same WLAN only one single shared key is used.

WEP can be used only once to encrypt transmittable data packets. In this case the Open System Authentication is used. The sending device encrypts the data with the configured cipher key. The receiving component uses the same cipher key to decrypt. Another variant combines WEP encryption with Shared Key Authentication.

Today WEP is heavily criticized, because the procedure does not bear up against serious attacks. There are programs like AirSnort [57] under LINUX and later WINDOWS that are capable to uncover keys used by WEP. A sufficiently large portion of data packets (5–10 million) has to be scanned to do the trick.

Stream Ciphers

The reason for the weakness of the WEP mechanism is basically the choice of the encryption procedure. The cipher key lengths in question are 64 and 104 bits with a 24 bit default. The user can thus only work with 40 and 104 bits respectively (that is why manufacturers talk about 40 and 104 bit encryption).

With 40 bits generally four keys are supported, which are generated by five groups of two hexadecimal values each like: Cd 55 63 EF 56. The cipher keys are either entered manually or created automatically. In the latter case cipher key generation is associated with a password.

WEP uses the RC4 [58] algorithm (Fig. 2.24). RC4 stands for Rivest Cipher No. 4, pointing to developer Ron Rivest, who also participated in the development of the RSA encryption method. This cipher is also called stream cipher – a random generator, which permits to generate a stream of ciphers of any length from a single secret cipher key with fixed length.

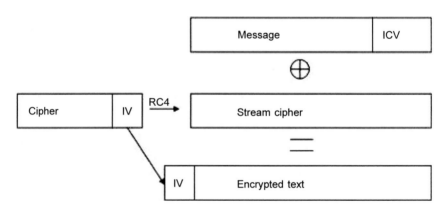

Fig. 2.24 The Functioning of WEP

The secret cipher key is combined out of a random initialization vector (IV) of 24 bits length and the 40 or 104 bits reserved for the access point. Before sending user data with a message a check sum of 32 bits length of the non-encrypted data will be created. This Integrity Check Value (ICV) is attached to the data. The cipher stream is generated with exactly the length corresponding to the adjusted user data length. Since the maximum length of such messages is limited to 2304 bytes the frame body can attain up to 2312 bytes with WEP.

Cipher stream and enlarged user data will be linked bit by bit to each other by XOR operations. The result is transmitted preceded by the IV. The receiver inverses this procedure and reconstitutes the original contents of the message. After decryption the check sum is generated once again and compared with the original value. Once the result is OK the data packet is accepted otherwise rejected. WEP only encrypts user data and the check sum but not management or control data.

Lack of Cipher Key Administration

Another weak point of WEP is cipher key administration or rather the lack of it. WEP only uses one single cipher key for all components in the same WLAN. This quite often means that secret cipher keys are never changed or only very rarely. And guest users need to know the cipher key as well to have access to the WLAN. On top of this some manufacturers of WLAN adapters store the key in such a way that it can be uncovered quite easily. Once a key has been uncovered or corrupted, because an untrustworthy person knows it, the whole network is in danger.

Many WLAN components actually in use still offer WEP in spite of its known weak points. Therefore one should at least ameliorate the situation by changing the WEP cipher keys more frequently.

Insufficient Cipher Key Length

The basic weak point of WEP was initially its 64(49) cipher key being to short to withstand attacks. Such cipher keys can be identified rather quickly with the assistance of programs by testing all possible bit combinations for the recorded messages under scrutiny. Quite often manufacturers aggravate this problem by generating the hexadecimal key only out of ASCII strings, reducing the number of variations even more. This brute force attack is now much more difficult for 128(104)-bit cipher keys.

Initialization Vector

Another serious weak point is the short length of the 24-bit initialization vector. The initialization vector is generated by the sender and should be different for each transmittable data packet. Components manufacturers should make sure these possibilities exist. This is not always taken care of, which means that the soft spot regarding the initialization vector persists.

Stream cipher operations can only be secure once the bit stream generated by the relevant algorithm differs between two data packets. With 24 bits a maximum of 2^{24} corresponding to 16.8 million cipher keys can be generated. Since some manufacturers only provide simple counters for the initialization vector the spectrum of randomly generated combinations is reduced significantly. But even, if a cipher key has been generated completely randomly the probability that a cipher key has already been used before is >50% after the transmission of 4823 data packets.

If there are two data packets within the same data recording using the same cipher key, an XOR operation applied to both encrypted texts could eliminate the cipher stream and reconstitute plain text. This is the entry point for decrypting other plain texts as well. This opens up the possibility to introduce data packets until the next cipher key change since the access point regards them as correctly encrypted.

Unreliable Authentication

Even the authentication protocol described above can be broken in a similar fashion, once an attacker records it, since both the authentication procedure and the user data use the same key. Another weakness in this procedure is its one-sidedness. A station has to prove its identity to an access point but not vice versa. Therefore a station does not have the possibility to find out, whether the expected access point is an unfriendly camouflaged access point.

2.7.7.6 *Better WEP than no Protection at All*

Even though WEP security can be broken by suitable means within a time span of hours an improved cipher key change frequency ameliorates the situation somewhat. Attackers would have to start over again to break the encryption. But in practice many users do not even use the insufficient WEP provisions since they are only optional.

The susceptibility of WLANs has been demonstrated by so-called war walking. Someone tries to detect unprotected WLANs via notebooks or PDAs from the outside. The intention is to use Internet access free of charge, spying on other people and to manipulate foreign data.

2.7.7.7 WPA and WPA2

To compensate for the weaknesses of WEP proprietary mechanisms like WEPplus or Fast Packet Keying [59] have been developed to implement better security procedures. The Wi-Fi Protected Access (WPA) procedure introduced by the Wi-Fi Alliance in 2002 has gained wider circulation.

TKIP

WPA uses a procedure called Temporal Key Integrity Protocol (TKIP) [60] developed by the Task Group for the later standard 802.11i. For reasons of downward compatibility the encryption algorithm RC4 has been maintained, but instead of a permanent cipher key temporary keys have been introduced. TKIP thus is basically an improved variant of WEP, comprising an extended initialization vector, dynamic cipher key generation and a cryptographic Message Integrity Check (MIC) also called "Michael".

2.7.7.8 802.1x [61]

Another option is 802.1x. This standard specifies user authentication and administration of cipher keys for LANs generally. For this purpose a special authentication server is necessary taking over the overall access control of the whole network. The server and its clients then exchange messages to identify themselves. Before successful authentication, neither the access point is able to accept data from a station, nor can a station receive data from the access point. Furthermore a special cipher key for this session is generated to protect the succeeding data traffic.

Authentication Procedure

802.1x offers a convenient way to establish cipher keys for WLANs to provide for typical encryption security. The authentication is access based in mobile Wi-Fi networks. Authenticators, integrated in wireless access points, are elements of the authentication system, which can grant or deny access. The user tries to get access to the WLAN via the authenticator, which in turn demands certification of credentials for authentication at the access point. Authentication servers belong to the RADIUS (Remote Authentication Dial-In User Service) server family.

The 802.1x process starts, when the user gets in touch with the authenticator to gain access to the network (Fig. 2.25).

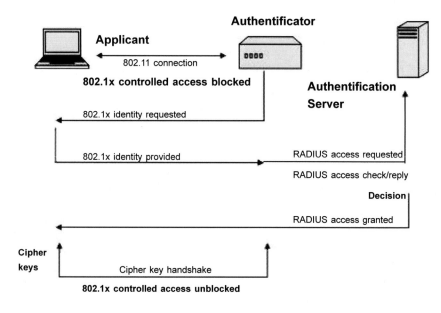

Fig. 2.25 The 802.1x Procedure

The system blocks all traffic of the client except what is necessary for authentication. Once the access attempt has been detected the authenticator demands the identity of the user.

The user identifies himself and his request to gain access to the authentication server via the authenticator. Thereafter an exchange of question and answer messages takes place with regard to the protocol. Sometimes the network not only authenticates the client, but the client itself tries to find out, whether the network it is trying to gain access to is trustworthy itself. This increases the question and answer traffic.

Once the user has met all conditions the server informs the authenticator to grant access. Thereafter user and authenticator exchange cipher keys.

Typically the user authenticates himself via one of the many EAPs (Extensible Authentication Protocols) [62].

IEEE 802.1x generates single user cipher keys for each session. This is to prevent problems related to some security techniques such as WEP, which need a decoding key for all terminals connected to the same access point.

When the user logs off, he sends a message to the authenticator, which resets the access to be blocked for any non-authenticated traffic.

Till today the standard 802.1x is not used extensively despite all its advantages. Reasons are to be found in relatively high investment and running costs. Organizations wanting to deploy the standard have to buy additional components and the RADIUS server, install and configure them. Many users are not used to that. The complex installation process costs time and money. On top of this the suppliers quite often provide their specific version of the standard, which are not always compatible between them. 802.1x can handle so many different authentication methods that users have problems to select the most advantageous.

The Open Sea Alliance [63] tries to solve these problems by developing open source reference installations to reduce the dependency on providers and operating systems. In this way they hope to obtain better interoperability and a wider use of the standard.

2.8 RECENT DEVELOPMENTS

2.8.1 White Spaces

The current frequency range permitted to be used for wireless communications lies between 2.4 and 5 GHz. However, within the overall spectrum of frequencies administrated by the FCC there are so-called white spaces: frequencies not used by anyone. They are situated between portions used by cable TV and telephone applications. The FCC now proposes to free those unused portions for use in wireless communications. This may open up services employing wireless broadband applications at low cost. White spaces are situated between 500 and 700 MHz. Because of these relatively low frequencies, those radio waves will not be attenuated as much as those currently in use by buildings or the atmosphere, reducing the usual dead communication zones. The challenge will be to develop an appropriate standard. This will take some time so that first products will not be on the market before a year or two from now [64].

2.8.2 The 802.11ac and 802.11ad Standards

Although much improvement concerning transmission rates has been achieved by releasing the 802.11n standard, consumer demands put more pressure on technology for even more throughput. Reasons can be found in video or home entertainment applications. This has led to the creation of working groups to develop two more standards: the 802.11ac and the 802.11ad.

2.8.2.1 802.11ac

802.11ac will be based on the classical 802.11a, thus operating in the 5 GHz frequency range. To make the standard work, transmission and receiving equipment will have to be upgraded with appropriate electronics. The available transmission channels will allow theoretical throughput of maximally 1 GBit/s. In addition the 802.11ac will transmit at lower frequency such that walls will be a lesser obstacle. As with other advanced standards encryption and authentication will be provided. As with the 802.11n channel bonding and MIMO features will be included.

2.8.2.2 802.11ad

In parallel to the 802.11ac the standard 802.11ad is being worked on. It will include similar features as the 802.11ac, but its range of operation will lie in the 60 GHz band. Its theoretical maximal throughput will be 7 GBit/s. The disadvantage is its small range such that it will be useful only within the bounds of a normal room. In total four channels of 2.16 GHz width will be needed, which is considerably wider than the 802.11n so that the 802.11ad can do without channel bonding. Using beam forming to increase the transmission rates will lead to higher frequencies which will, however, prevent passing through walls [65].

2.8.3 Mobile Hotspots

Up to now hotspots are offered as a service in a fixed location for users passing by or explicitly relying thereon. Considerations now go into the direction of personal mobile hotspots, which could be carried around by individuals. So, even, when there is no traditional hotspot available, people could still connect, if they wanted to.

Mobile hotspots are such devices as routers with uplinks, which can be battery powered, and provide security features such as encryption and authentication. The devices already on the market use the traditional 802.11a and 802.11g standards, but the fast 802.11n is considered as well [66].

2.9 APPLICATIONS

2.9.1 A Small Home WLAN

Figure 2.26 shows a typical example of a small private WLAN, which can be assembled in any household. All that is needed is a

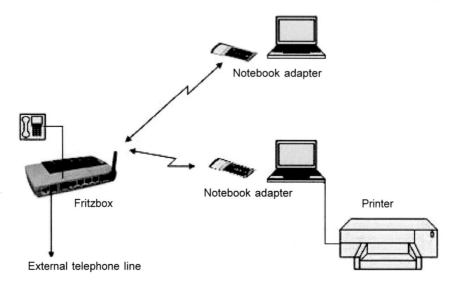

Fig. 2.26   A Small Home WLAN

router (in this case a Fritzbox) connecting to a private telephone line with DSL capabilities. The two laptops are each equipped with a notebook WLAN adapter. One of the stations has a locally connected printer. The adapters send out signals to search for the emissions of the Fritzbox [67] router. Once the lock on the frequency connection is established, the network is in operation. Note: The notebooks do not communicate directly with one another in this example.

2.9.2   Hot Spot Services

Figure 2.27 shows the setup of a hot spot service center acting as intermediary between two public WLANs, the Internet and a company network.

2.9.3   WLAN Solutions for a Hospital

WLAN solutions for hospitals can be extensions of existing LANs. This allows for access to patient and hospital data anywhere in the premises and in all areas – especially, where traditional

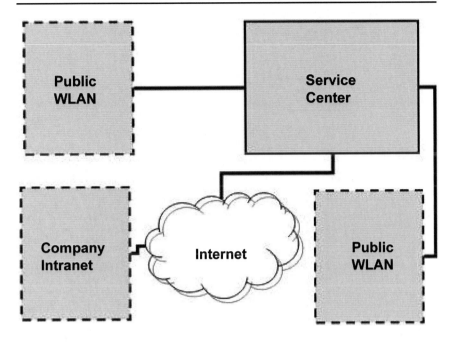

Fig. 2.27 Hot Spot Service Center

cabling is difficult to arrange. In any case personnel becomes more flexible thus increasing their efficiency. New applications like store management for pharmaceuticals, mobile ward rounds or IP telephony via WLAN are additional possibilities.

Information access is no longer dependent on specific locations. This enhances cooperation between personnel working in different areas. Unified communications, enhanced security functions (interface to central radio linked alarm systems) and to localization services are possible. Further applications include local resource management concerning free bed or room capacities or medical equipment. These data can be mapped to a graphical display of the hospital floor plan. Via the radio linked alarm system nurses can place emergency calls or track the movements of disabled patients.

2.10 CHECKLIST

Table 2.3   Checklist For WLAN Implementation

Do you want to set up and operate a WLAN?	When setting up and operating a wireless network additional security aspects compared to a cable network have to be taken into account.
Do you plan a WLAN in a large organization?	In a large organization a WLAN has to be integrated into the total IT strategy including the IT security strategy.
Would you like to set up a small private network?	The technical challenges are basically the same as in an organization; only the formal aspects of IT security management are not relevant.
Does a formal IT security management exist in your company?	IT security management deals with all security aspects, when setting up and running IT installations.
Are the terms of reference for security management documented?	Precondition for a functioning IT security management is a sound documentation.
Are the prevalent security standards taken into account for your security management?	For WLAN ISO 17799 among others is relevant.
Are security criteria documented?	Security is classified according to confidentiality, availability, integrity, etc.
After security instructions do participants have to sign a declaration?	Participation in security instructions should be documented in the interests of all concerned.
	Signatures are at the same time legally binding and constitute additional commitment to the organization.
Is compliance to security regulations checked regularly?	Compliance should be checked according to a master plan.
Is WLAN operation documented as part of IT security management?	WLANs can pose significant security risks and thus their operation has to be integrated into the overall IT strategy.
Do rules exist in your company against uncontrolled growth of WLANs?	Quite often WLAN initiatives are started by advanced users; they have to be integrated into the overall management concept.

Table 2.3 Contd. ...

	Unauthorized utilization of other networks via WLAN access offers an uncontrolled gateway for external attacks.
Are the types of data to be handled by a WLAN specified?	According to security classifications certain company data belong to different security classes.
	Transfer of confidential data should only be possible in encrypted form.
Does a WLAN user guide exist?	A WLAN user guide is part of the IT security documentation.
	Missing guidelines for WLAN utilization lead to uncontrolled growth in an organization.
Do general conditions for authorized WLAN access exist?	The general conditions include training, commitment to the company security standards, usage of hotspots, etc.
	Uncontrolled WLAN access undermines the internal security standards.
Do WLAN guidelines exist for system administrators?	These guidelines determine rules for configuring and operating WLAN components.
Do documents for WLAN training exist?	These documents should also contain security requirements besides technical aspects.
Are administrators and users trained concerning WLAN security?	Because of the increased security risks in connection with WLANs detailed knowledge of the major weak points are of prime importance.
Are WLAN components part of the data backup strategy?	Backup strategy is part of the overall documented IT security strategy and of the operating manuals.
	WLAN components should have special attention within the overall backup strategy.
Are data stored on WLAN components part of the general backup?	WLAN components can carry all relevant configuration data for operation besides the usual business data.
	WLAN components may contain configuration data as well as business data, both of which have to be safeguarded.
Does the WLAN security directive undergo regular revisions?	Regular revision of IT security directives – especially for WLANs – is part of the internal security process in an organization.
	State-of-the-art techniques and standards for components vary rapidly requiring regular updates of a directive.

Table 2.3 Contd. ...

Has a contingency plan been developed?	Security incidents concern attacks on WLANs or LANs via a WLAN to spy data, deposit data, to falsify information, to erase them and to steal WLAN components.
	According to the type of security incident a standard process should be triggered as a specific reaction.
Do contingency plan and error handling constitute part of WLAN instructions?	Different security incidents require adapted reactions to be documented as a process if possible: immediate technical measures, documentation, reporting channels, strategic countermeasures, etc.
Does a proper configuration management exist in your company?	Only the configuration management for WLANs should be allowed to set up the components according to the standards in use in the company while respecting the security directives.
Have the WLAN standards to be employed been decided upon?	The market offers different standards: IEEE 802.11b, 11g for the 2.4 GHz band; 11a, 11h for the 5 GHz band e.g. a company should use one single standard.
Has a standard configuration been developed?	To support WLAN components efficiently a standard configuration should have been developed according to security directives.
Is configuration done in wireless fashion?	WLAN components can be configured via cable or in wireless fashion.
	Configurations should not be done wireless if possible to avoid the spying of passphrases and cipher keys.
Is the default password of the manufacturer for routers routinely and immediately replaced?	Routers are generally provided with a password by the manufacturer.
	Included default passwords can be identified without problems in the Internet and therefore should be replaced as a first configuration measure.
Do you employ an individual SSID?	The default settings by the manufacturer of SSIDs should be changed from the onset.
Does your SSID designation enable inference about the user?	Descriptive designations may indicate the area of utilization and therefore the data material.

Table 2.3 Contd. ...

	The SSID designation must not enable inference about usage to avoid additional incentives for spying.
Is the broadcast of beacon frames of the SSID suppressed?	The broadcast of the SSID indicates to the environment that a WLAN is active.
	The spying on active WLANs with the intention to penetrate is called war driving. This is facilitated by SSID broadcasts.
Is your radio link encrypted?	Encryption of radio links is one of the basic measures to prevent attacks from the outside.
	Authentication data and confidential information should be transmitted only in encrypted mode.
Are radio links regularly checked with analytical tools?	Analytical tools allow the detection of successful or attempted non-authorized accesses.
Is access to networks regulated in general?	Access to WLANs and LANs should be regulated by processes conforming to audit standards.
	Unregulated access and links bypass organizational measures of the IT security management.
Do you reduce your transmission power to the minimum necessary?	On the one hand a certain transmission power is required to operate the system; on the other hand this can be a security risk.
	The limitation of transmission power prevents intensive broadcasts and thus the detection of a WLAN operated within the boundaries of a company.
Do you use an Access Control List (ACL) when employing RADIUS servers?	The utilization of the IEEE 801.1x standard allows for additional authentication of users via an Access Control List (ACL); the authentication is routed via a centrally controlled RADIUS server.
Have the locations for the installation of WLAN components been determined?	The geographical location of WLAN components determines the broadcast to the outside and prevents dead spot problems.
	WLAN components can suffer interference from radio waves originating from other technical appliances preventing their operation in the vicinity of them.

Table 2.3 Contd. ...

Is the ad hoc mode always switched off?	The ad hoc mode allows the setup of a spontaneous WLAN by client to client communication.
	When the ad hoc mode is switched on unauthorized clients may access the WLAN directly.
Do you switch off the Dynamic Host Configuration Protocol (DHCP), if you use it?	DHCP server automatically allocates IP addresses for the overall network.
	DHCP can be a gateway for attacks by allocating a valid IP address to an intruder in the worst case.
Are the frequency channels in use selected without overlapping?	If the frequency channels are to close to each other this can lead to interferences.
	Interferences can be avoided, when channels are used that are far enough apart at any one time thus having a channel separation as wide as possible.
Is your network checked for dead spots?	Dead spots are created by interferences from other electromagnetic waves, an inadequate geographical arrangement, badly adjusted antennas or insufficient transmission power.
	Analytical tools allow the detection of dead spots otherwise being experienced by users as disruptions.
Are WLAN components switched off when not in use for some time?	To avoid unnecessary broadcasts WLAN components not in use should be switched off.
	Broadcasts indicate to external spies and war drivers that a WLAN is in operation.
Do you use WEP encryption technology?	WEP encryption technology uses a symmetrical process providing access points and clients with a common key.
	WEP encryption technology is generally regarded as unsecure, but should be preferred against not encrypting at all.
Do you use WAP encryption technology?	The possibilities of the WAP process are state-of-the-art today. If employed they should be applied to all network components.

Table 2.3 Contd. ...

	Larger networks should be protected additionally by a RADIUS server with Access Control List administration.
Do you use the IEEE 802.1x mechanisms?	IEEE 802.1x is a framework standard using a RADIUS server.
Do you take care to avoid weak passphrases?	The security of passphrases depends on their length and character combination.
	Weak passphrases are short, consisting only of alphabetical letters and can be found in dictionaries.
Do you use authentication methods relying on reciprocity?	With these methods clients and server exchange information to authenticate themselves (IEEE 802.1x)...
Do you use the preshared key method?	With the PSK method for each user cycle a new cipher key between client and access point is generated.
Do you use WEP in contexts with confidential information?	WEP encryption technology uses a symmetrical process providing access points and clients with a common key.
	WEP encryption technology is generally regarded as unsecure, but should be preferred against not encrypting at all.
Do you use WAP2?	WAP2 refers to the standard IEEE 802.11i – an improvement with regard to WAP employing the Advanced Encryption Standard (AES).
Are encryption options checked when buying new components?	When selecting new components it is important to buy those with the highest standard present in the network.
Are cryptographic keys replaced regularly?	To prevent systematic spying keys should be changed on a regular basis.
	The key change should proceed according to a fixed time table. Change should take place once per months, at maximum once per quarter.
Does your company have a dedicated data protection management?	Data protection management deals with integrity, confidentiality, availability and access security for all data in store in a company.
Are confidential data encrypted on mobile devices?	When using mobile terminals certain data have to be stored locally on the devices.

Table 2.3 Contd. ...

	Mobile devices run a higher risk of theft and loss. If confidential data have to be stored locally they should be encrypted.
Are internal and external networks defined, to which links may be established?	WLANs can act as a gateway to linked LANs.
Is the WLAN linked to a LAN?	In a linkup between WLAN and LAN the WLAN is the weakest spot against external attacks.
Do you employ security gateways when accessing a LAN from a WLAN?	In many cases the security level of a radio link and its components does not correspond to that of a LAN.
	The high security requirements for the transition from WLAN to LAN can be realized with a security gateway.
Does the possibility exist to block WLAN communication from the LAN?	At the point of transition a total blocking of the WLAN communication should be made a possible option, if required.
Do you operate access points as hotspots?	Hotspots facilitate a wireless and simple access to the Internet.
	When operating access points as hotspots additional security measures are necessary especially when operating a LAN in the same configuration.
Are hotspots connected to a LAN?	In a WLAN to LAN linkage it is possible to gain access to a LAN via a hotspot.
	Hotspots should be connected to a LAN only through a security gateway.
Is inter-client communication permitted?	Inter-client communication allows the setup of an ad hoc network without integrated control devices such as access points or routers.
	Inter-client communication should generally not be permitted in permanent networks.
Do you have a protection strategy against viruses, worms and Trojan horses?	Most organizations employ special software to scan incoming data against infection.
	The protection strategy against infection should have the same level as that for LANs.

Table 2.3 Contd. ...

Are your installations protected by firewalls?	A firewall controls data traffic between network segments and the outer world on different communication layers.
	When working with the Internet firewalls are an indispensable part of the security strategy.
Are provisions taken to safeguard the network against technical disturbances?	Technical disturbances can originate from different devices emitting radio signals: microwave ovens, surveillance cameras, etc.
Do you employ WLAN management systems?	WLAN management systems document the configuration, analyses network operation and deals with incidents.
Do you document the results of security checks?	This documentation can be handled by a WLAN management system.
Do you analyze the security relevance of these results?	The analysis results should be documented in a WLAN management system.
Are there regular audits?	Audits consider configuration parameters, access rights, password cycle, and compliance with security directives.
	Audits are necessary because of changing technologies and personal turnover.
Do you employ WLAN analysis tools?	WLAN analysis tools check the installations against unauthorized WLAN operations, find dead spots and evaluate signal quality.
Do you employ penetration tests?	Penetration tests simulate attempts of unauthorized access to the network and thus provide a measure for access security.
Are cross points and authentication server checked regularly?	Checking the functioning of those components is part of a regular system audit.
	Cross points and authentication server are critical components regarding network attacks.
Do you regularly check your clients with respect to their configuration and being up to date?	Especially when security standards have been raised one has to make sure that clients comply.
Do you verify the employment of non-authorized components?	Checking against non-authorized components is part of the security audit.
	Besides using a WLAN analysis tool physical verification of devices should be done as well.

Table 2.3 Contd. ...

Have measures defined to protect the network against interferences?	Interferences can be avoided by carefully selecting locations or by switching off or displacing the sources of disturbances.
Do you document disturbances or abnormalities?	All disturbances and security incidents should be documented with the help of a WLAN management tool.
	Analysis of error messages permits the recognition of attack patterns or systematic security loopholes.
Is it possible to access the Internet from the WLAN?	Unprotected Internet access is a favorite target for attacks to a WLAN.
	Internet access has to be protected by a security gateway.
Is hotspot usage regulated?	Once terminals have been equipped with WLAN adapters access to freely available hotspots is possible.
	The usage of hotspots can be prevented by technical means.
Is the usage of external WLANs restricted?	External WLANs allowed to be accessed should be defined in the security directive.
	Access rules to these networks should be defined amicably with the owner of these networks.
Are appropriate encryption methods employed for data transmission between hotspots and server?	Hotspot operation permits simple wireless Internet access for external users.
	Besides the security provisions given by WLAN standards web authentication and additional protocols for data encryption should be employed.
Is there a master plan after theft of critical components?	Measures have to be taken to prevent that stolen components continue to allow access. All configuration data relating to security have to be replaced within the total network.
Do you have a directive for decommissioning WLAN components?	When decommissioning WLAN components at a minimum all configuration data have to be erased.

3

PDAs

3.1 OTHER WIRELESS TECHNOLOGIES

The widespread use of so-called handhelds has produced the option that PDAs have a real potential for mobile access of centrally administrated applications in organizations. These devices can be bought by anyone at reasonable prices, for example, via mobile phone contracts. This, however, has led to new types of security risks. Of course the potential risks already outlined for WLANs in general are still the same, but others, completely new ones, have been added to the list. And others in turn have aggravated already identified weak spots. Before discussing the whole spectrum of these risk potentials and the ways and means to control them, an introduction into the system environment of these devices is necessary.

Up to now only the classical network components (with the exception WMAN) and their interactions have been introduced in depth: servers, routers, PCs, laptops and their related adapters. In the meantime additional terminal devices, which can be integrated into a WLAN, have entered the market. These will be discussed in the following sequence:

- hardware
- standards
- configuration
- security aspects

3.2 HARDWARE COMPONENTS

Three components will be looked at. The following explanations take care of operations in a classical WLAN. Other protocols such as Bluetooth or UMTS will be dealt with later in the book. These components comprise:

- PDAs
- BlackBerries [68] as a special type of PDA and only briefly
- Printers

Especially the first two of these have gained increasing importance with respect to the classical laptop connections. The old and new risk potentials will be presented further down. Initially basic functionalities will be presented.

3.2.1 PDAs

As of today the market offers a rather confusing multitude of different types of PDAs (Personal Digital Assistant) [69] (Fig. 3.1). As such this corresponds to the choice of mobile phones as well. At this stage, however, the telephone functions of PDAs will not be discussed. When selecting a PDA the following criteria are of importance:

- weight
- size
- ease of handling and
- capabilities.

To be considered as well are different combinations of operating systems and interface protocols. These criteria can be differentiated further to meet either the requirements of individual users or to facilitate strategic decision making within a company, about which type of device is most suited for their applications:

- type of application and/or
- ease of handling.

Fig. 3.1 PDA

3.2.1.1 Types of Applications

Nowadays applications are as multifaceted as there are functions in organizations. One has to differentiate:

- between local and networking functions on the one hand, and
- between typical PDA functions and other functions within a company.

Typical examples for both categories are:

- utilization of office software
- telephone
- organizer
- contacts management
- media management
- navigation systems
- email functions and Internet
- data management

- application specific to a company in connection with WLANs
- other programs

The advantage of PDAs with respect to classical terminals such as laptops or deck tops are obvious: while traveling or being otherwise outside the company infrastructure – in meetings for example – many functions can be executed just by carrying such a small and habile device. This even surpasses the mobility advantages of a laptop. Its weight is small. There is no need for a special transport case. On top of this these devices offer a multitude of options for private use (as a function of price and facilities offered):

- GPS [70]
- navigation systems
- photographic data handling
- MP3 player
- videos etc.

It is, however, obvious that the limit between serious and business oriented usage and – just as with the use of the Internet – gimmickry can be overstepped easily. And here the sources for security hazards are to be found. To minimize those a maximum of discipline is required by all parties concerned.

It is a fact that most types of PDAs are offered within a price category that is no obstacle for the average mobile phone user. For the moment the mobile telephony with PDAs will be excluded from our considerations, since it will be discussed in a later chapter.

3.2.1.2 *Modalities if Use*

Many individual users think that the handling comfort is as important as the system functions offered when selecting a particular device to buy. Concerning the first criterion one important difference is to be found in the basic philosophy as to how input is managed:

- with keypad or
- without keypad.

Concerning PDAs without keypad there are further variants. These include input possibilities either via

- touch screen or via
- pen and display.

IT strategists and IT security officers in companies, however, have more important selection criteria than individual users, who want to cater to their own private gimmick interests besides executing professional functions. Strategic considerations comprise such criteria as outlined in Table 3.1.

Table 3.1 PDA Selection Criteria

Criteria
ease of maintenance and software updates
integrated backup facility
user friendliness
battery lifetime
purchase price
running maintenance costs
configuration parameters and synchronization
interface to central systems
support of communication standards
authentication possibilities

The emphasis of each individual criterion depends of course on the planned use of the PDA in connection with company functions and problems associated with usage in a WLAN for example.

Initially the first generation of PDAs did not have effective storage protection. Today, however, the present generation offers virtual storage handling and multi-tasking capabilities. Besides this there are possibilities for data encryption and authentification interfaces. And there are separate data management systems.

3.2.2 BlackBerries

BlackBerries are really only a very specific type of PDA brought on the market by the company Research in Motion (RIM) [71]. However, they constitute a category on its own, which offers their own specific possibilities of usage and therefore also of security risks. The manufacturers, being aware of this, provide for appropriate security concepts. These will be discussed separately.

BlackBerries enhance classical PDA functionalities significantly (Fig. 3.2). A BlackBerry is primarily used for the exchange of emails and PIM (Personal Information Management) data. For this purpose it uses a special real time operating software with its own proper communication protocol. Its additional mobile telephone capabilities will be discussed later.

Fig. 3.2 Blackberry

Besides functional and ergonomic ones a BlackBerry offers additional advantages with respect to other PDAs. For example, all data are kept synchronously between server and terminal as long as the connection is alive. Its integrated Mobile Data Service (MDS) [72] provides for easy access to internal company data bases. Another feature comprises the compression of large quantities of data with the help of the BlackBerry Enterprise Server (BES) [73], which transports these as data streams onto the terminal under acceptable performance. For this special encryption mechanisms are provided for.

At the same time a BlackBerry terminal is capable to join other internal communication systems within a company via the BES and Instant Messaging facility.

Ergonomically the device can be operated with one hand only because of its track wheel and the arrangement of its touch buttons. The more recent versions have dispensed with the track wheel and are equipped with a sure type touchpad.

BlackBerries are capable to operate within an existing server architecture within an organizations. Thus a degree of complexity is attained, which asks for corresponding management tools. A special platform with these necessary tools has been developed:

- push software applications for specified user groups
- version management
- specific security modules
- monitoring possibilities.

Today all these functions can be executed via one single administrator console – under standard WINDOWS © operating systems and firewall protection.

Information concerning the security philosophy of BlackBerries are to be found later on.

3.2.3 Printers

Printers can be connected and addressed wirelessly via a WLAN with the help of different protocols and technologies. The printers must have all necessary adapters and must be placed in a location favorable to receive wireless signals and not in dead spots.

Once a printer is equipped with the required 802.11g/b interface and has a reasonable reach of 50 m, for example, checks have to be carried out, whether security functions like WPA, password protection, allocation of MAC addresses etc. are available. WLAN configuration is done via the usual menu navigation for peripherals.

It is important to note that WLAN printers also transmit continually their presence, so that an attacker from outside would notice a printer and therefore a WLAN´s existence. Appropriate security measures have to be implemented.

3.3 STANDARDS

There are a number of standards that can serve the needs for administrators or procurement operators. For the following it is assumed that Wi-Fi has been accepted as the dominant wireless technology. Thus only a brief summary of the relevant Wi-Fi standards useful for the operation of PDAs in WLANs will be given.

3.3.1 802.11b

The 802.11b is the oldest standard. It is stable and is supported and in use widely. A network under 802.11b has a theoretical processing speed of up to 11 Mbit/s. In praxis though the throughput lies at 5 Mbit/s maximum. Advantages of this standard are in the relatively low price segment and in its widespread compatibility. 802.11b hardware can be found anywhere and does not cost very much in comparison to 802.11g for example.

There are, however, also drawbacks: security and performance are two of them. Security is a problem, because the 802.11b is nowadays so widely used, that to this day there are sufficient tools around to enter any 802.11b network by anyone, who is determined enough.

One source concerning performance problems is the radio frequency. Meanwhile there are so many access points around. It is not unusual that interferences with other access points within a certain geographical sector can occur. Since the 802.11b operates within the 2.4 GHz band, interferences with other microwave appliances are also possible.

3.3.2 802.11g

802.11g is an enhancement of 802.11b. Therefore it too operates within the 2.4 GHz frequency bandwidth. Thus the interference problems are similar to 802.11b. Its main advantage, however, is its transmission rate, which is situated at a maximum of 54 Mbit/s. Again these advantages are met with some drawbacks.

Firstly, an 802.11g signal requires a bandwidth of 30 MHz, whereas the totally available bandwidth corresponds to 90 MHz. This means that within one and the same configuration in a given area only three access points can be operated at the same time.

Another advantage of the 802.11g besides its speed is its advanced compatibility – among others also backwards to the 802.11b. Thus an upgrade from 802.11b to 802.11g is unproblematic. Table 3.2 summarizes the important characteristics of the two standards.

Table 3.2   802.11x Standards

Standard	Transmission Rate [Mbit/s]	Frequency Range [GHz]	Reach [m]
802.11b	5-11	2.4	inside 20-40 outside 30-100
802.11g	54	2.4	inside 20-40 outside 30-100

3.4 CONFIGURATION

The following assumes that there is already a functioning WLAN within an organization, which has been optimally configured in the past.

3.4.1 Access Points

At first the default parameters of the manufacturer have to be replaced by the organization's own security settings to avoid unauthorized access.

The connection of an access points to a PC is either done directly with the help of a crossover cable or by a switch or hub in a cable network (Fig. 3.3). This is the sequence of configuration.

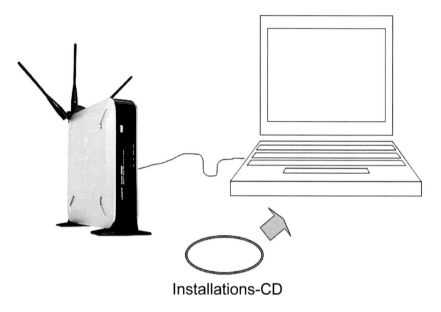

Installations-CD

Fig. 3.3 Connecting an Access Point

Switch on access point and start the installation CD. The setup assistant searches the network for access points. Depending on the manufacturer either a new SSID will be allocated or an automatic IP address allocation will take place. Other relevant security aspects will be discussed later on.

3.4.2 PDA Adapter

There are PDAs on the market, which already have adapters integrated. If this is not the case, one has to find out whether the PDA is equipped with a CF (Compact Flash) [74] interface or not. If it is, the WLAN CF adapter can be inserted into the relevant slot.

These adapters usually also provide power management features. They support all common 802.11 standards. On top of that they are normally compatible with Pocket PC 2002 or higher. They operate within the 2.4 GHz spectrum and support a data transmission rate of up to 54 Mbit/s. Generally 128-bit WEP encryption possibilities is provided for (Fig. 3.4).

Fig. 3.4 WLAN-PDA Adapter of Linksys

The following describes briefly the configuration steps required:

3.4.2.1 *Preparation of the PC*

Pre-condition for the installation is a suitable synchronization software like ActiveSync from Microsoft ©. (Normally one can purchase such a software on CD, when buying the PDA itself.) Once the synchronization software has been implemented the setup, which has been delivered with the CF card, can be started. PDA and computer are initially connected via cable. It is important that the CF card has not been inserted into the PDA at this stage. Prior to this the setup installation has to be started on the PC. This is done with the usual user navigation, which consists of nothing but a sequence of acknowledgements in the course of the installation run ("yes", "next", "ok", "exit"). After successful installation the configuration proper can commence.

3.4.2.2 Configuring the Adapter Card

The connection between PDA and computer has to be cut now. After this the adapter card has to be inserted into the PDA. Thereafter the start menu will appear on the PDA display. It asks for the confirmation of the proposed IP address. After confirmation the logo of the WLAN monitor will appear on the PDA display.

3.4.2.3 Connection

The next step is the activation of the wireless icon on the PDA by clicking on it. Now the configuration options are proposed for selection. Further steps depend on the PDA operating system.

3.4.2.4 Example PC 2003 (Microsoft©)

To start with the WLAN, with which the communication has to take place, has to be selected. In case of WEP authentication the designated cipher key has to be keyed in. After this the connection will be completed. In case of no WEP authentication the connection is done automatically (by "ok" input).

3.4.2.5 Example PC 2002 (Microsoft©)

For this particular case the configuration menu offers several access points for selection. The administrator is requested to enter the network name in the SSID field. In case of WEP security the cipher key has to be entered in hexadecimal format. There are additional options concerning power management. To use them their effect on reach and performance have to be taken into account.

3.4.3 Integrated WLAN Functions

Many PDAs support integrated WLAN functions. They offer a variety of menu guided configuration options:
- display of availability of a WLAN in the vicinity (continuous search option, even when using other functions)
- selection of operating mode: infrastructure or ad hoc
- selection of access points

- selection of security mode: WEP, WPA
- definition of cipher keys.

3.5 SECURITY ASPECTS

PDAs present additional security risks to the general classical risks already discussed for WLANs. Therefore dedicated enhanced countermeasures are necessary. These risks will be outlined in the following in detail. Before that decisions have to be taken already at the strategic level, when attempting network design. Basic issues have to be addressed. Only an efficient interplay between organizational and technical measures will succeed in minimizing the overall risk (Fig. 3.5).

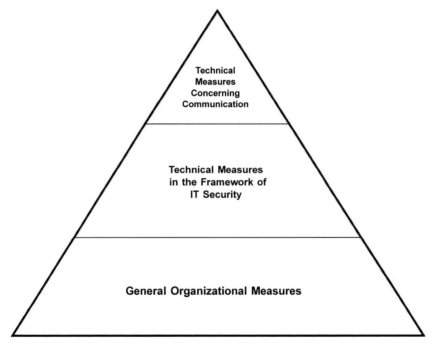

Fig. 3.5 Security Pyramid

A precise and detailed catalogue of measures is structured according to criteria proposed in Table 3.3:

Table 3.3   Security Risks

Scenario	Target	Type of Attack
attacker in possession of the device	applications	theft
	services	manipulation
attacker does not possess the device	operating systems	
	communications	
	infrastructure	

3.5.1   Basic Security Risks

Mobile terminals are prone to be operated in insecure environments. The reason lies in the nature of their simple mobility itself. On top of that their different communication protocols and interfaces to many operating systems offer plenty of targets for determined intruders. Some devices do not have elaborate security functions. PDAs can be stolen, get lost or damaged easier than laptops or PCs that are installed in a fixed location.

Besides this PDAs possess the usual soft spots, which are common in general in relation with wireless communication, such as:

- eavesdropping potential
- sometimes too simple authentication procedures
- sensitivity against intended or unintended interfering signals.

In addition there are the classical targets that can also be found in wired networks (sneaking in via the Internet, through email accounts etc.).

3.5.2   Strategic Countermeasures

As already mentioned, a certain minimization of the risk potential can be achieved upfront with respect to the actual productive application operation by devising a suitable implementation strategy for PDAs. For this a number of basic issues have to addressed, such as:

- Which are the applications suitable for the deployment of PDAs?

- Will these specific terminals be provided by the organization or are private devices considered as well?
- Which data will be permitted to be stored on the PDAs?
- Does the organization have clear and mutually agreed directives covering the usage of PDAs as part of their security strategy?
- Do appropriate control mechanisms exist to largely exclude unauthorized usage.

Once these basic issues have been addressed, the persons responsible can start thinking of selecting the devices to be purchased. Table 3.4 lists some criteria, which could be of use in the selection process.

Table 3.4   Selection Criteria for the Procurement of PDAs

Criteria
ease of maintenance, update strategy of the manufacturer
system stability, backup procedures
user friendliness
size and weight
price
initial implementation and configuration
administrator interface
data transmission protocols

With the help of such a catalogue of criteria the market can be explored. Additionally the selection criteria can be weighted to simplify the decision making. Special emphasis should be placed on the following security aspects:

- authentication procedures
- encryption possibilities for data transmission
- imbedding of additional security features through updates for example
- data backup facilities

All these aspects suggest that the procurement should be done in agreement with the technical experts in the organization.

3.5.3 Organizational Countermeasures

Organizational countermeasures can be differentiated with respect to:

- general organizational countermeasures
- technical countermeasures in conjunction with IT security
- technical countermeasures concerning communication.

All these requirements can be grouped together as a separate branch in its own right of the overall IT strategy of an organization. They ought to be documented in a suitable form.

3.5.3.1 General Organizational Countermeasures

The following measures have to be documented. The users have to be instructed accordingly. Their acknowledgement has to be certified by signature and to be archived (Fig. 3.6). These are the measures:

- control of private terminals regarding their usage in conjunction with the company WLAN.

Generally the usage of private PDAs should be excluded – both concerning internal company application as well as data synchronization.

- clearance procedure for applications to be executed by terminal devices

Only certified software intended for usage in the company is allowed to be deployed on PDAs. Everything else must be excluded: from games to ring tones.

- encryption specifications for communication and data

The IT security department has to provide an encryption algorithm to be employed by the users. Although security requirements have to be met, this algorithm should at the same time be simple to use.

- Commitment to physical control of the mobile devices

The commitment for controlling includes the requirement to securely store the devices. This exceeds a company's premises, when carrying the device while traveling or taking it home. These rules do also apply for airplanes or underground car parks. When

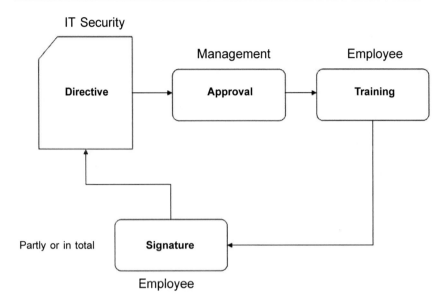

IT Security

Fig. 3.6 Directive Process

the devices are not in use, they should either be carried along or locked away safely.

- Directives for data backup

IT security has to specify the procedures and the frequency concerning the safeguard of certain data stored on a PDA by the user himself.

- Restrictive operation outside the organization

PDAs lend themselves for usage also outside a company. This is one of the main advantages why PDAs are bought in the first place. The distinctive disadvantage can be found in all the security problems already mentioned above. Therefore such external usage should only be cleared for applications, where the advantages outweigh the combined security risks.

3.5.3.2 *Technical Countermeasures: IT Security and Communication*

- Inventory of the devices

Although, because of their purchase price certain PDAs can be regarded as low value assets, the technical inventory is the basis for a close monitoring of the devices. The inventory should always contain the name of any current user of a particular device.

• Password strategy

The password strategy comprises two aspects:

– definition of the password replacement cycle

– definition of password structure: length, combination of characters etc.

• Encryption of data and storage media

To be able to implement the above mentioned organizational measures for data encryption IT management has to select a procedure to be implemented by the users easily.

• Authentication concept

The authentication concept for PDAs should exceed the already existing general concept for applications. For this personal authentication of the user at the PDA level should be required even before system logon in addition to WLAN authentication itself, logon protection for applications and other functional restrictions on applications (Fig. 3.7).

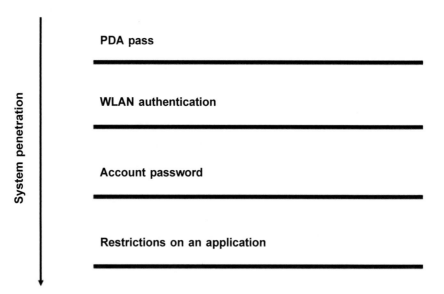

Fig. 3.7 Authorization Layers

- Synchronization with secure protocols

From usage of applications or checking business emails apart synchronization of calendar functions belong to the attractive features of PDAs. This can be achieved either by a wired connection or wireless. If the latter way is chosen one has to make sure that the transmission protocols in use are sufficiently secure to avoid or impede eavesdropping by unauthorized persons.

- Embedding devices into existing operating systems without plug-ins

Downloading plug-ins to, for example, increase the user friendliness of established operating system programs or for the purpose of customizing should not be allowed and – if possible – prohibited by technical means (administrator rights).

- Monitoring identification and authentication transactions

By appropriate logging and preserving log files for a sufficient length of time such transactions can be traced later on – including abortive attempts by would-be intruders.

To make all the measures work relevant control modalities have to be introduced – for example:

- Network control software (Sec. 3.5.3.3)
- Alerting mechanisms

Outside technical measures, which correspond to those for a WLAN independent of PDA deployment (disabling access etc.), theft and loss of a PDA require additional action. For this purpose an organization should have implemented a proper alerting process. It could be structured along the lines proposed in Figure 3.8.

- Regular check of infrastructure

IT security together with IT management are responsible for documenting the existing infrastructure. They are also required to check their sustainability. This includes – besides physical inspections – the monitoring of all relevant communication protocols and log files and to identify accesses from stations, which do not have official clearance. Because building layouts or the geography of the operational area can change as a result of internal removals the physical conditions for a continuous optimal network communication have to be verified regularly.

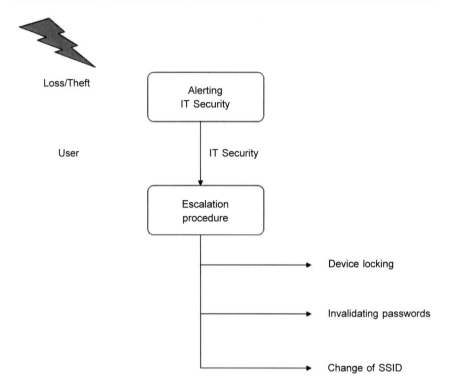

Fig. 3.8   Alerting Process

- Update of synchronization programs, communication protocols and operating system software

These software components have to be kept at the latest technical level to guarantee continuous compatibility on the one hand and support by the provider on the other. A fallback behind the latest release level minus two is not acceptable.

3.5.3.3   *Network Access Control (NAC)*

There are a variety of offers on the market with different levels of depth. In all cases logging is the basis to register successful but also failed attempts to enter the network. At the same time these programs make it possible to obtain information about the user status within the network at any time: number of users logged in, number of processes running, data traffic etc. Besides this it is possible to activate access filters at IT or MAC level.

NAC Software provides authentication, end point security, access control checking and monitoring of behavior. Basically a NAC front end checks any connection attempt to a network. It then determines, whether the user is authorized. Using a more sophisticated algorithm, such as PDPs (Policy Decision Points), the NAC software combines logical user information with device identity (Fig. 3.9). From its result, the system determines, which level of access may be granted. At the same time, remote devices are checked, whether they have their own security provisions installed [75].

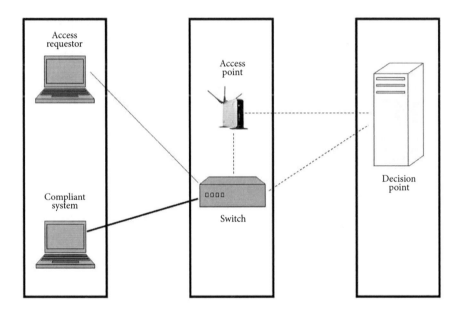

Fig. 3.9 PDP

After initial verification NAC systems continue to monitor user behavior on an ongoing basis.

3.5.4 Specific Risk Potentials

The specific risk potentials have been outlined at the beginning of this section in Table 3.3. Now the two scenarios

- "attacker in possession of the device" and
- "attacker does not possess the device"

will be detailed with respect to the consequences for:

- applications
- services
- operating systems
- communication and
- infrastructure.

3.5.4.1 Attacker in Possession of the Device

This is the most serious scenario. The following security potentials can be identified:

Target of Attack: Applications

- spying on data: personal data, data relevant to security and configuration, business data
- manipulation of data including deletion: undermining competitiveness of a company by falsifying and sabotage
- gathering information about company processes: about workflows, about data bank structures, and email folders
- analysis of the operating system, checking security parameters: the acquisition of this information allows deeper penetration into the companies data world
- manipulation of registry: altering system parameters in a LAN in such a way that usage will be impeded or made impossible
- introducing viruses etc.

Target of Attack: Services and Operating System

- analysis of operating system, security parameters (Sec. Target of Attack: Applications)
- manipulation of registry (Sec. Target of Attack: Applications)
- introduction of viruses etc.

Target of Attack: Infrastructure

- manipulation of the terminal device in such a way that abuse will not be detected immediately

- destruction of the device
- copying and deployment of an alien device: pretending legal access

3.5.4.2 *Attacker does not Possess the Device*

This is more difficult for the attacker. But a technically accomplished attacker is still capable to wreak damage by using other means to gain access with the help of an alien device. This requires prior eavesdropping on the PDA communication traffic with appropriate technology. These are the security risk potentials:

Target of Attack: Applications

- spying on data
- manipulation of data including deletion
- gathering information about company processes
- analysis of operating system, security parameters
- manipulation of registry
- introducing viruses etc.

Targets of Attack: Services and Operating System

- hacking of authentication codes: by eavesdropping on the radio traffic getting hold of the authentication codes
- using creeping-in methods to get into sessions; then
- operating system analysis, security parameters
- manipulation of registry
- introducing viruses etc.
- denial of service: creating massive load on servers that are used for routing messages thus bringing the whole system to a standstill – in other contexts a favorite method to block Internet pages

Target of Attack: Communication

- spoofing: all attempts to get hold of authentication codes, network protocols, and system addresses

- man in the middle camouflage: introducing oneself between two communication partners and by this means gaining knowledge of all important information to successively penetrate and spy on a system
- denial of service by pursuant usage of services
- protocol attack: manipulating protocols and mappings and thus rendering systems useless
- eavesdropping, sniffing

Target of Attack: Infrastructure

- theft of the terminal device
- eavesdropping on data traffic to deduce the infrastructure of an installation (Sec. Target of Attack: Communication)

3.5.5 Special Case BlackBerries

The manufacturers of BlackBerries, RIM (Research in Motion), have developed a whole panoply of security mechanisms, which come with the system. These comprise:

- a holistic security concept for organizations
- special encryption algorithms
- exceptional security measures for WLAN message transmissions
- exceptional protection for the component architecture
- local user authentication
- facilities for device control
- special measures after theft or loss.

In this book some exemplary aspects will be followed up.

3.5.5.1 The Overall Security Concept

The BlackBerry solution is based on the Symmetric Key Cryptography [76]. This method insures confidentiality, integrity and authenticity.

Confidentiality is assured by encryption based on a secret cipher key, which is known only by the intended receiver.

Integrity is achieved by a random process. The BlackBerry device sends data together with one or more message keys generated randomly to avoid decryption by third parties. Only the BlackBerry Enterprise Server and the device itself have knowledge of the master key and the format used.

Authenticity is guaranteed through authentication of the device by the BlackBerry Enterprise Server using this master key.

Maximum data protection is achieved by

- encryption of all data traffic between the BlackBerry Enterprise Server and the terminal device
- encryption of data traffic between the message server and the email system of the user
- encryption of data on the terminal device itself
- encryption of configuration parameters
- local user authentication on the device by a smart card with password or passphrase.

3.5.5.2 *Security in WLANs*

The BlackBerry security concept attempts to harmonize advanced security approaches with existing network technology. The aim is that the end user can send and receive messages without problems in a secure environment without being bound to a particular workplace. The interplay with a BlackBerry Enterprise server functions along the lines outlined in Fig. 3.10.

X sends a message to Y from his desktop. X and Y work in the same company.

The message server receives the email and informs the BlackBerry Enterprise server about the reception.

The message server delivers the message to the desktop of Y.

The BlackBerry Enterprise server takes the message from the message server.

The BlackBerry Enterprise server queries the message server, if the forwarding function for the mobile BlackBerry of Y has been enabled.

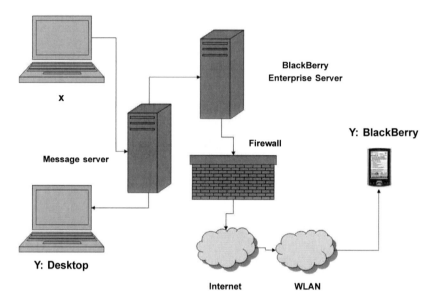

Fig. 3.10 Reception of a Message on a BlackBerry

The BlackBerry Enterprise server packs and encrypts the message.

The BlackBerry Enterprise server puts the message into the sending queue.

The WLAN routes and delivers the encrypted message to the BlackBerry of Y.

The BlackBerry of Y receives the encrypted message, decrypts it and displays it.

The reverse process – sending a message from a BlackBerry inward – goes along similar lines (Fig. 3.11).

Y sends a message from his BlackBerry via the WLAN.

The message is transmitted via the Internet.

The message has to pass the firewall of the central network.

The message arrives on the BlackBerry Enterprise server.

From there it is forwarded to the message server.

Finally it appears on the desktop of X.

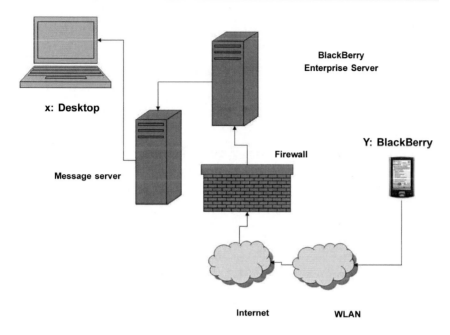

Fig. 3.11 Internal Message Processing

3.5.5.3 Theft or Loss of BlackBerries

There are a number of countermeasures, which are suited to trigger certain security mechanisms even after a BlackBerry has got into the possession of unauthorized third parties. These include:

- protection of applications by passwords
- detection of accesses from logfiles
- restriction of download possibilities
- locking of the device
- remote disabling and deletion of certain data as soon as an access attempt has been started from the stolen device
- deletion of master keys
- decoupling of the smart card from the device.

3.5.5.4 Management Platforms for BlackBerries

To save costs and to increase security management, platforms have been developed for large size BlackBerry applications. These management systems fulfill the following requirements:

- pushing of specific software applications to certain users or user groups
- administration of versions, upgrades and group memberships
- detect, notify and delete non-authorized applications on individual BlackBerries
- support and administrate thousands of BlackBerry users and a multitude of BlackBerry Enterprise servers
- user logging, authentication and analysis.

These functionalities are the basis for status reports dealing with the following queries:

- What does the BlackBerry infrastructure look like?
- Which applications are in current use?
- What kind of software is implemented on the terminal devices?
- What activities are currently going on on these devices?
- How many devices of which type are in use?

3.5.6 PDA Directive

One of the organizational measures to improve security in a corporation, when using PDAs on a large scale, is the drafting and enforcement of appropriate directives. Such a directive should contain the following elements:

- description of objectives
- definition of scope
- policy concerning the authorized usage of PDAs
- consequences by noncompliance
- approval and signature

3.5.6.1 Objectives

The PDA directive is the basis for cost control, organizational security and prevention of theft of PDA devices.

3.5.6.2 Scope

This directive applies to persons in charge on all management levels (executive board, managing directors, heads of departments etc.), all employees carrying PDAs, employees of subcontractors, part time workers, apprentices and other employees getting in touch with such applications.

3.5.6.3 The Directive

The following is a draft example of such a directive:

Directive for the usage of PDAs

The company provides PDAs for a limited number of users. To obtain a user license a special application has to be filed (PDA application form). After assessment a license may be granted.

In exceptional cases superiors may apply for PDAs for their staff members. This is possible, if compelling business requirements can justify this. The application can be filed informally to the IT security officer.

The Management of the IT department is responsible for the selection of compatible PDAs and for organizing their support. Decisions concerning user authorization do not fall within its field of competence, which is also the case for the provision of the necessary financial means for the procurement of individual devices. Costs for purchase and maintenance of PDA usage have to be borne by the different departments themselves.

PDAs, which belong to the company, may only be used for purposes in connection with the company's business. Any personal usage is excluded. Expenses that occur through personal usage by the user have to be borne by the user himself. Expenses that occur for the company through such personal usage will be billed by the company to the user.

It is prohibited to install non-authorized software on company PDAs. It is equally prohibited to download additional software or services (ring tones e.g.) on PDAs.

It is forbidden to dock non-authorized PDAs onto other company devices such as computers, laptops, servers or networks, to connect with them or synchronize with them without prior written permission.

Employees, who obtain a usage license, are responsible for the security of these devices. The devices have to be carried along permanently throughout a business trip. Stolen or lost PDAs will have to be replaced by the user. The devices remain property of the company.

Sensitive and confidential information may not be stored on the PDA. In case of loss or theft the IT security officer has to be informed without delay to trigger the necessary steps for remote deletion of contact, calendar and configuration data.

Non-compliance

Any non-compliance incident against this directive has to be notified to the IT security officer. Non-compliance may lead to disciplinary sanctions up to the dissolution of the employment contract. This is independent from other legal actions."

Acknowledgement of the Instruction

This directive should be part of comprehensive employee security instructions. Thereafter the following agreement can be signed:

Acknowledgement of the PDA Directive

"Please read the present PDA directive and countersign it at the bottom of the document. One copy with your signature will be kept by the IT security officer.

With your signature you acknowledge:

1. I have received the PDA directive, understood its meaning and agree with it.
2. I confirm that I will use PDAs handed out to me by my employer exclusively for the company's business activities.
3. I agree that I shall carry all costs, which may occur for the company as a consequence of my private use.

4. I will not connect PDAs to computers, laptops, servers, systems or networks, which have not been cleared for this.

5. I will not store confidential and security relevant data on the PDA.

6. I understand that I am responsible for the security and replacement of the device after loss. The device remains the property of the company.

7. I understand that non-compliance regarding this directive can induce legal consequences.

>Name
>
>Signature
>
>Department
>
>Date"

A PDA directive cannot exclude any risk on its own. It is therefore important that the IT security officers follow up the strict enforcement of the directive. This goes together with the already mentioned technical measures and the application of suitable management platforms.

3.6 CHECKLIST

Table 3.5 lists all aspects with relevance to security, when using PDAs in a WLAN.

Table 3.5 Checklist PDAs

Does A WLAN already exist in your work environment?	When operating a wireless network additional security requirements have to be observed with respect to a cabled LAN.
Do you want to build a new WLAN?	In major organizations a WLAN should be part of the overall IT strategy including IT security strategy.
Are the responsibilities for security clearly regulated (strategically. organizationally, technically)?	The organizational security procedures can be differentiated with regard to general organizational measures, technical measures concerning IT security, technical measures regarding communications.

Table 3.5 Contd. ...

	Unresolved responsibilities endanger regular operations.
Have security directives regarding WLAN usage been documented?	Security directives constitute a separate area of a company's IT security strategy.
	Security aspects with regard to WLANs should be documented separately.
Do the security guidelines contain a catalog of countermeasures in case of security incidents?	Depending on the type of incident different countermeasures take effect.
Has the usage of handheld devices been regulated?	Besides the already existing security risks in WLANs handhelds constitute completely new types of risks.
	High mobility and additional communication potentials increase security risks significantly.
Do control mechanism exist to exclude unauthorized usage?	A suitable deployment policy for handhelds can minimize the security risks.
	Missing control mechanisms can lead to unauthorized and undiscovered usage.
Have authorized network functions been defined for handhelds?	Communication protocols and interfaces to operating systems offer plenty of opportunities for determined attackers.
	Network functions should be limited to the absolute necessary.
Have email functions been defined for handhelds?	Any account structures should be specified beforehand.
	Email traffic should be reduced to the necessary.
Are there directives for local data storage?	Organizational concepts for data encryption should be provided by IT management as technical procedures.
	Data backup strategy should not be left to the discretion of the end user.
Do procedures for storage protection exist?	Motives for attack are among others spying on and manipulating data including deletion.
Are data encrypted?	Encryption of data and storage media is a basic part of security strategy.

Table 3.5 Contd. ...

Do agreed procedures for data backup exist?	IT security has to advise on procedures how end users themselves have to backup certain data residing on terminals.
	Data backup should be controlled centrally.
Are business applications of the company executed from handhelds?	There has to be a general decision which applications should be allowed to be executed from handhelds.
Do clearing procedures exist for applications on terminals?	Only software for company needs and certified for this purpose should be allowed to go on stream for PDAs.
	Clearing procedures have to be defined together with IT security.
Is private usage of company handhelds permitted?	Private usage of company handhelds should be excluded if possible.
	Private usage lies outside the controllable function areas.
Are private terminals permitted to be used in the companies WLAN?	Private terminals should only be allowed in exceptional cases.
Do control mechanisms exist concerning deployment and usage of private terminals in the company?	Usage of private terminals should be subject to mandatory control mechanisms.
	In exceptional cases private devices may go online under defined conditions.
Have selection criteria been defined for the purchase of these terminals?	A catalog of criteria is useful to sound the market. Special attention should be given to security aspects.
Does an authentication interface exist?	The provision of an authentication interface should be a major procurement criterion.
	Without authentication interface no WLAN should go into operation.
Have the terminal devices been tested with respect to resilience?	Resilience should be a procurement criterion.
	Low resilience endangers operations.
Is the update strategy of the manufacturer known?	Only the most recent and secure releases should be deployed.

Table 3.5 Contd. ...

Have PDAs been deployed or will they be?	PDAs are a real option for the mobile usage of central applications in companies.
Do you differentiate between typical PDA and other company functions?	One has to differentiate between local and network related functions and between typical PDA and company functions.
Are PDA adapters protected by WEP technology?	Today WPA procedures have been introduced to IEEE 802.11n and are state-of-the-art now. If deployed this should be made possible for all network components.
	WEP technology is regarded as unsecure, however, should still be used, if there are no other provisions available.
Have BlackBerries been deployed or will they be in the future?	BlackBerries are really only a special type of PDA, which have been introduced to the market by Research in Motion (RIM).
Do you use RIM specific functions?	Besides functional and ergonomic ones BlackBerries offer additional advantages with respect to regular PDAs.
Does a well-defined BlackBerry server infrastructure exist?	BlackBerries can be operated in companies and other organizations within a suitable server infrastructure.
Do you use Mobile Data Service for accessing company data bases?	BlackBerries integrated MDS (Mobile Data Service) facilitates simple access to company data bases.
Is a BlackBerry Enterprise server used for encryption?	The BlackBerry solution is based on Symmetric Key Cryptography. Only the BlackBerry Enterprise server and the device itself know the Master Key.
	All security features delivered with the BlackBerry should be activated.
Do you use Instant Messaging functions?	The BlackBerry terminal is qualified to participate in other company communication systems via the BES and Instant Messaging.
Are BlackBerries subject to a strict version management?	The BlackBerry Management Platform offers management functions to administrate versions, upgrades and group memberships.
Is the BlackBerry security concept in use?	The BlackBerry security concept combines advanced security features with existing network technology.

Table 3.5 Contd. ...

	All security features delivered with the BlackBerry should be activated.
Is data traffic between the BlackBerry Enterprise server and terminals encrypted?	The BlackBerry device sends one or more messaging cipher keys generated by a random procedure to prevent decryption by third parties.
	Data should never be transmitted without encryption.
Is data traffic between the message server and the email system encrypted?	Encryption of data traffic is achieved between the message server and the users email system.
	Data should never be transmitted without encryption.
Are data on the BlackBerry itself encrypted?	Encryption of data can take place on the terminal itself.
	Stored data should also be encrypted if possible.
Is a local user identification by Smart Card, password or passphrase required?	BlackBerries offer local user authentification features at the device level by Smart Card with password or passphrase.
Is it possible to decouple the Smart Card?	BlackBerries facilitate decoupling of Smart Cards from the device.
	Decoupling is an additional security advantage.
Are applications protected by password?	Individual applications can be protected by passwords.
	Protection by passwords are a matter of course.
Are security mechanisms defined in case of theft?	There should be mechanisms, which are suited to trigger countermeasures in case of theft.
	Theft of handhelds represent the highest level of risk.
Is logging analysis carried out regularly to control access?	The BlackBerry Management Platform permits user logging, authentication and analysis.
Have downloads been restricted?	Restriction of downloads can be achieved by organizational and technical means.
	This should also be the case for ring tones.
Does a possibility exist to block devices?	Some device types carry locking mechanisms.

Table 3.5 Contd. ...

	Nearly all regular devices have such possibilities integrated as a standard.
Does remote disabling exist?	Remote disabling and deletion of certain data should be carried out in case of an authorized access attempt from a stolen device.
	Remote disabling should be executed immediately after theft.
Does the possibility exist for remote deletion of data?	Remote deletion prevents unauthorized access to application data.
	Remote deletion of all data should proceed immediately after theft.
Can master keys be deleted remotely?	After remote deletion of master keys unauthorized authentication can be prevented.
	Master keys are gateways for all kinds of attacks.
Do you use the management platform for BlackBerries?	To reduce costs and to increase security management platforms are on offer for major BlackBerry applications.
Are printers accessed via WLAN?	Printers can be connected and driven by various protocols and technologies via WLAN.
Is WPA technology used when operating printers?	WPA features have been introduced in IEEE 802.11 and are state-of-the-art today.
	Even for printers the most advanced security technology should be deployed.
Are MAC addresses used for printers?	MAC addresses are required for entry in the Access Control List.
Are printers protected by passwords?	Even for printers password protection does exist.
	Password protection prevents unauthorized access.
Is the IEEE 802.11b employed?	The IEEE 802.11b is the oldest standard. It is stable and widely supported and in use.
Is the IEEE 802.11g employed?	802.11g is an enhancement of 802.11b and therefore operates in the 2.4 GHz frequency band as well.
Are the default security parameters changed for access points?	First of all the default parameter setting of the manufacturer have to be replaced by proper ones.

Table 3.5 Contd. ...

	Default settings are known publicly.
Do you use power management features?	Power management can influence the reach.
Are countermeasures against eavesdropping in place?	Only by an efficient combination of organizational and technical measures can the overall risk be reduced.
	Eavesdropping for some length of time may reveal even encrypted passwords and data.
Are authentication procedures employed?	Authentication procedures are the main prerequisite for WLAN security.
	Without authentication procedures no WLAN should be operated.
Are authentication and identification procedures subject to control?	By appropriate logging and storage of log files over a longer period transaction can be reconstructed later – including failed attempts by intruders.
	Logging permits the detection of attack attempts.
Have technical countermeasures been devised against interference from outside?	Interferences may originate from physical causes, for example, from other devices emitting radiation.
	By appropriate geographical placement technical interference can be avoided.
Are terminal devices inventoried?	The IT security officer together with IT management is responsible for documenting the existing infrastructure.
Is the infrastructure checked regularly?	This comprises physical inspection as well as checks on all relevant communication protocols and log files.
	Checking the records should follow a regular schedule.
Is a password change strategy in place?	The change strategy comprises the rate of change as well as the password format.
	Change strategy should not be left to the discretion of the users.
Has a password change cycle been defined?	For the change cycle a time schedule should be communicated. Change should take place either monthly or at most quarterly.

Table 3.5 Contd. ...

	Passwords should be supplied with an expiry date.
Are complex password structures required?	The security of passphrases depends strongly on their length and character combination.
	Simple passwords can be guessed by an attacker easily.
Does an authorization concept exist?	The authorization concept for PDAs should go beyond any already existing application concept.
	The security documentation should contain a coherent authorization concept.
Is calendar synchronization protected by secure protocols?	Apart from using applications or email querying synchronization of agenda functions are part of a PDA's attractive features.
	When synchronizing the possibility of accidental downloading of viruses etc. has to be excluded.
Are plug-ins permitted?	Downloading of plug-ins to increase the user friendliness of regular operating system functions or for purposes of customizing should not be allowed and if possible be prevented by technical means.
	Plug-ins change the nature of accepted applications.
Is network control software employed?	The programs provide information about the user status of the network at any time: number of users, number of processes running, traffic etc.
Do alert procedures exist in case of security incidents?	Any organization should have a suitable alert process in place.
	Without any alert process timely intervention is not to be guaranteed.
Will synchronization programs and communication protocols be updated regularly?	These software components should be kept at the most recent level to warrant continued compatibility and support by the manufacturer.
Is there any obligation to physically control terminal devices?	Employees having received handhelds with authorization to use them are responsible for the security of these devices.
Does a directive for data backup exist?	Such a directive is the basis for cost control, organizational security and the prevention of theft of PDA devices.

Table 3.5 Contd. ...

	Data security directives are integral part of the overall security documentation.
Are the terminal devices distributed restrictively for use outside the company?	The company provides handhelds for a limited number of users. To obtain a general user clearance a proper application has to be filed.
	Private usage should be restricted because of security and costs.
Does a separate PDA directive exist?	This directive applies to all those responsible on all levels, all employees of subcontractors, part time workers, apprentices and other employees.
	When deploying PDAs such a directive is indispensable.
Will employees be committed to take note of the PDA directive?	This directive should be part of a comprehensive security training of employees. In the end an appropriate agreement should be signed.
	Every PDA user should be instructed and countersign the instruction.

4

Mobile Phones

4.1 CONTEXT

The previous discussion concerning WLAN security have centered around classical terminal devices with their corresponding architecture (laptops, PCs, printers). Additional aspects have been addressed in connection with PDAs. These included new risk potential and corresponding security strategies. PDAs and BlackBerries, however, are also mobile phones. This functionality has been excluded until now. This part shall cover security risks in connection with the usage of mobile phones in its proper sense.

Although PDAs are a subclass of mobile phones the risk potentials so far covered have only taken into account their usage in WLANs. Of interest for further considerations is the fact that mobile phones pose a risk in serving as gateways for attacks on central applications, when employing either their communication functions or certain services that come with these devices. When using a mobile phone both for telephony and WLAN applications at the same time, additional risk potential arise, which will be discussed in more detail in this section, even though this technology is still in its initial stages. Thus there is no way to circumvent any aspect of mobile telephony.

Firstly the architecture of mobile phones will be looked at. On this basis current operating systems will be introduced briefly. These operating systems may include various services relevant to security considerations. So there will be again specific threat scenarios and corresponding countermeasures to protect installations.

Just in the previous chapter for PDAs here again the special case "BlackBerries" shall be dealt with. Other special cases are Smart

Phones and – more recently – iPhones [77]. And finally a directive tailored to the specific requirements for mobile phones in general will be presented.

4.2 BASIC PRINCIPLES

One has to distinguish between:
- external communication structure and
- internal device architecture.

The interplay between both may lead to situations, where security management becomes important. However, even the pure existence of a mobile phone poses a security risk in itself. To understand this, the basic principles of communication and device architecture and its functioning will be presented in the following.

4.2.1 Communication Structure

The general structure of a mobile network is laid out in Fig. 4.1.

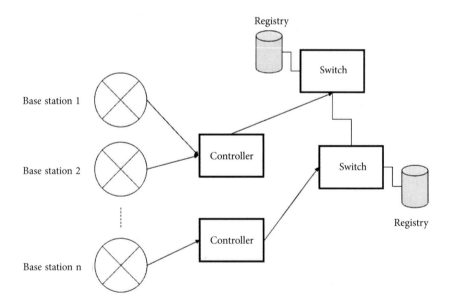

Fig. 4.1 Structure of a Mobile Phone Network

What can be seen is a cellular network in its hierarchical arrangement. The main components are:

- the phone itself
- base station
- control unit
- transmitting station and
- switching node.

Provider and end user are connected via the base stations. Base stations can serve several cells. They themselves are managed by the control units. Routing and service switching are carried out by the switching node. Additionally a number of registers for the administration of subscribers are required. This will be discussed further down.

It is important to note that there is normally no end-to-end connection between mobile phones themselves – in contrast to certain terminal devices in WLANs – since the communication is routed via the network.

The deployment of a mobile phone for WLAN communication is shown in Fig. 4.2.

It is evident that two different protocols are required. The solutions currently on the market do not necessitate a route via the mobile phone net. Mobile phones equipped for such communications can directly connect with a WLAN via an access point.

4.2.2 Device Architecture

Nowadays mobile phone have similar capabilities as PCs. Surpassing their initial functionalities for voice communication they are equipped with far more applications. These capabilities carry costs in terms of security risks since the user now possesses additional degrees of freedom. Manufacturers have taken this into account by including in their basic configuration functional modules and a separate security module. The functional modules can be separated into

- the communications part and
- local applications.

Fig. 4.2 Mobile Phone in a WLAN

The main local security module centers around the so-called SIM (Subscriber Identity Module) card [78]. The following items are stored on this card:

- customer ID
- IMSI (International Mobile Subscriber Identity)
- dial number
- authentication data.

- The physical separation of SIM and device allows the usage of different devices by one and the same end user, since he can carry the SIM card along. The logical connection of the user is therefore to his SIM card and not to the device itself.

Figure 4.3 shows the typical architecture of a mobile phone with its various interfaces.

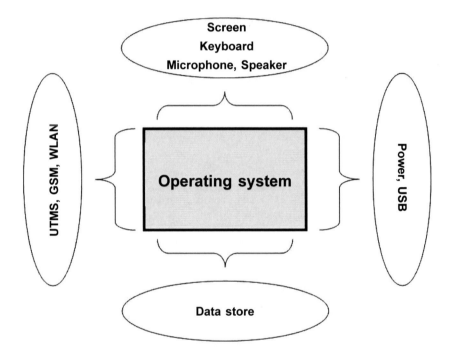

Fig. 4.3 Mobile Phone Architecture

There are four different types of interfaces:

- user
- communication
- storage medium
- devices.

Each type represents different targets for attack and of relevance to security. The various risk scenarios for these interfaces will be discussed further down.

4.3 OPERATING SYSTEMS

The operating systems of mobile phones support different communication techniques and protocols. In addition to simple standard functions other functions such as data management and file systems may come along. Integral part of all operating systems are cryptographic procedures and access control to protect the device and communications. The following popular operating systems will be introduced here:

- GSM [79]
- GPRS [80] and
- UMTS [81].

4.3.1 GSM

Figure 4.4 shows the communication schema for GSM.

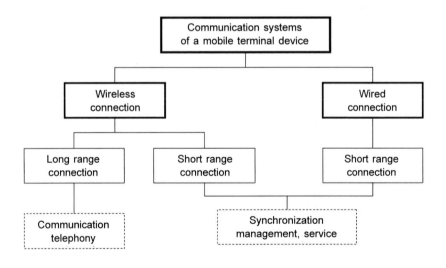

Ref.: BSI

Fig. 4.4 GSM Communication Schema

The whole network is subdivided into cells. These cells are served by base transceiver stations (BTS). They function as interfaces between the provider and the end user at the same time. Furthermore there are base station controllers (BSC) managing the resources of the BTS. The BTS are in turn controlled by mobile switching centers (MSC). The MSC take care of the classic routing including all processing even to fixed networks. In addition there exist a number of registers containing information, without which routing would not function:

- HLR/Home Location Register: information about subscribers (ID, services etc.)
- VLR/Visitor Location Register: status of the subscriber
- AUC/Authentication Centre: information relevant to authorization validation
- EIR/Equipment Identity Register: list of all approved terminal devices.

4.3.1.1 HSCSD [82]

HSCSD is an enhancement of GSM permitting the usage of several GSM radio channels at the same time. This increases the potential data transmission rate.

4.3.2 GPRS

GPRS can bundle several radio channels and is most suited for data transmission from the Internet for example and for sending emails. For this specific services have to be employed, for example, i-mode or WAP (Sec. 4.4.2 and 4.4.3).

4.3.3 UMTS

UMTS (Universal Mobile Telecommunications System) represents a new generation of mobile phone operating systems. Because of its optimized transmission mode more elaborate data formats besides text and voice can be transmitted at a high rate: video, Internet etc. This possibility offers additional services, but also represents new sources for risks.

4.3.3.1 HSDPA [83]

A further enhancement within UMTS is the HSDPA standard, which is most suitable for WLAN applications.

4.4 SERVICES

Apart from classical telephony today one can distinguish between the following additional services:

- general information services
- other communication services
- data transmission features

Figure 4.5 illustrates these user services schematically, build into the specific architectures.

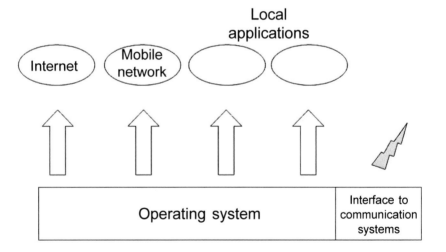

Fig. 4.5 User Services

The more important features are:

- SMS/EMS/MMS
- WAP and
- i-mode.

4.4.1 SMS/EMS/MMS

Theses abbreviations stand for:

- Short Message Service (SMS) [84]
- Enhanced Message Service (EMS)
- Multimedia Message Service (MMS).

The basic service is SMS. This service allows for transmission of text messages only. On its basis EMS and MMS have been further developed later on.

With EMS messages may be transmitted that exceed the text limit of SMS (160) as well as simple graphics. MMS now opens up for possibilities to send photos and short videos by mobile radio.

All three formats have in common that the messages are not routed directly to the receiver. The addressee gets a notification that a certain message is ready on call. Only once the addressee executes his call he will get the actual message, which is buffered on the server of the provider.

4.4.2 WAP [85]

WAP means Wireless Application Protocol. This service secures the transmission of information from the Internet. To be able to use this service the terminal devices have to be equipped with suitable browsers. The WAP architecture corresponds to those of other data networks as can be found in regular client server constellations.

4.4.3 i-mode [86]

i-mode represents yet another Internet access possibility via mobile radio and is therefore in direct competition to WAP. To use its functionality fully terminal devices have to be specially equipped.

4.5 MOBILE PHONES AND WLAN

As described mobile phones communicate via the discussed protocols. These also provide for the billing mechanisms. The future, however, points into a different direction. Concepts developed for these purposes aim to integrate both mobile phones and WLAN, so that mobile phone access can be realized using WLAN technology like access points or hotspots. But this also means additional security risks.

These service are currently handled under FMC (Fixed Mobile Convergence) [87] and UMA (Unlicensed Mobile Access) [88] (Fig. 4.6). To implement such services on a large scale a number of technical preconditions have to be created. These concern the terminal device on the one hand and the necessary infrastructure on the other.

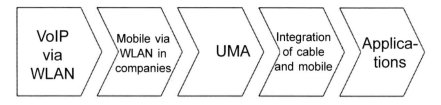

Fig. 4.6 Mobile Phones and WLAN Possibilities

4.5.1 Infrastructure

Concerning the infrastructure these are the areas of interest:
- convergence of voice networks and WLAN
- implementation of the relevant networks in organizations
- provision of the required services by mobile network providers
- integration of back office systems
- completely integrated media architecture with all relevant added value services.

Figure 4.7 shows a possible scenario integration of WLAN with UMA.

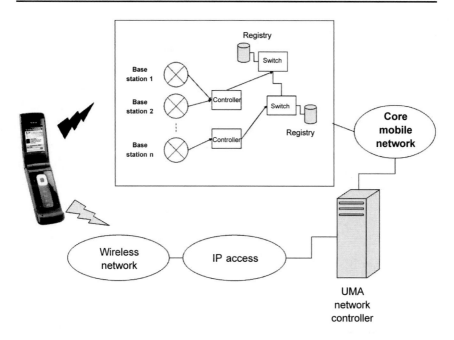

Fig. 4.7 UMA Architecture

4.5.2 Terminal Devices

Meanwhile the manufacturers of mobile phones are several steps ahead. After some hesitation concerning billing aspects the first phones with WLAN capability have appeared on the market. These have been enhanced accordingly and are also capable of VoIP (Sec. 4.8.2). They are usually also equipped with special touch screens or keyboards. There is still technological improvement required because of high electricity consumption leading to frequent recharges of the accumulators.

4.6 THREATS AND PROTECTION

4.6.1 General Risk Potentials and Strategic Countermeasures

Security risks emanating from mobile phones surpass largely the classical risks of typical WLAN applications. This is independent from the fact whether they are used for WLAN applications themselves (currently under development) or for telephony only. This means that most dangers are not really dependent from the type of usage but are part of the nature of the device. For all those reasons countermeasures are necessary that will surpass those mentioned about dangers created by PDA usage in a purely WLAN environment. These additional risk potentials will be identified in the following. As usual first measures have to be decided upon on the strategic level. For this purpose the importance of the interplay between strategic, organizational and technical measures is reminded upon (Fig. 4.8).

For mobile phones the following general catalogue of risk potentials is important (Table 4.1).

Table 4.1 Security Risks for Mobile Phones

Scenario	Target	Type of Attack
attacker in possession of the device	applications hardware device characteristics infection	theft
attacker does not possess the device	services DoS operating system communication infrastructure	manipulation

Besides general measures for all regular mobile phone applications manufacturers provide specific strategies, which will be presented further down with the example of BlackBerries. Just as outlined for PDAs the following is important for mobile phones as well:

- Contrary to wired terminals mobile terminals are prone to be operated much more often in unsecure environments.
- Besides the technical possibilities to spy on wireless traffic there is a soft spot, which is based on the nature of a mobile phone itself: acoustical eavesdropping.

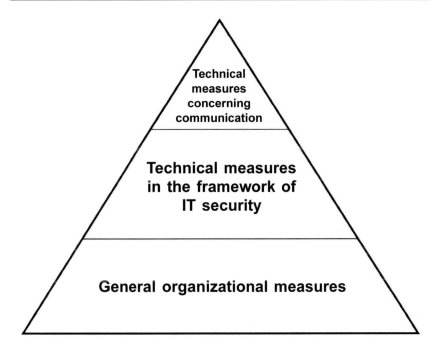

Fig. 4.8 Security Pyramid

- Authentication procedures for mobile phones are simple. In most cases a four-digit code suffices to not only gain access to the network under the recorded subscriber identity, but also to locally stored data on the device.
- Besides this all other points of attack known from WLANs and classical wired networks continue to exist.

4.6.1.1 *General Organizational Measures*

The organizational measures, which are of particular importance to the mobile phone sector, comprise:

- Regulation of the usage of mobile phones by directives such as the one already proposed for PDAs, to be modified accordingly.
- Definition of prior procurement criteria with respect to security in addition to those relevant to functionality and costs only.

- Enforcement of security regulations in an organization, if not already in place (such a strategy should in any case already exist for classical applications in every organization).
- Development of an authorization concept including a password strategy for mobile phones as well.
- Encryption concepts for data storage and all data traffic.
- Implementation of an alerting process in case of theft or loss of a terminal device including the detection of attempts to gain access illegally.

4.6.1.2 General Technical Measures

General technical measures comprise:
- Monitoring private terminal devices concerning their usage for company functions – especially in company WLANs.
- Clearance procedures for applications on terminal devices.
- Encryption guidelines for communication and data.
- Commitment for physical supervision of mobile terminal devices.
- Directives for data backup.
- Restriction for usage outside the company.
- Inventory of the devices.
- Development of an authentication strategy.
- Encryption of data and storage media.
- Development of an authorization concept.
- Synchronization only through secure protocols.
- Integration of the devices into existing operating systems without plug-ins.
- Monitoring of identification and authentication transactions.
- Deployment of Network Control Software.
- Alerting mechanisms.
- Frequent check of the infrastructure.
- Update of synchronization programs, communication protocols and operating systems.

4.6.2 Specific Threat Scenarios Concerning Mobile Phones

The following refers to the risk potentials outlined in Table 4.1 above. The two scenarios

- "attacker in possession of the device" and
- "attacker does not possess the device"

will be dealt with separately.

Attacks taking place under both conditions have impact on:

- applications
- services
- operating systems
- communication
- infrastructure
- hardware
- device characteristics
- infection and DoS

The relevant mobile phone specific situations present themselves as follows:

4.6.2.1 Attacker in Possession of the Device

This is the most dangerous scenario. In this context here once again a summary of the equivalent risk analysis for PDAs:

- spying on data: personal data, data relevant to security and configuration, business data
- manipulation of data including deletion: undermining competitiveness of a company by falsifying and sabotage
- gathering information about company processes: about workflows, about data bank structures, email folders
- analysis of the operating system, checking security parameters: the acquisition of this information allows deeper penetration into the companies data world
- manipulation of registry: altering system parameters in a LAN in such a way that usage will be impeded or made impossible
- introducing viruses etc.

In addition to those the following aspects are pertinent:

In the first place an attacker has at his disposal a panoply of technical possibilities to circumvent authentication routines. By this he not only enters the device itself but he then has all the options to penetrate internal and external applications. In any case he has a new launching pad for getting into network applications belonging to a specific organization. He has surmounted a first obstacle. Using further technical means he can try to conceal his illegal access by manipulation in a way that network administrators or communication officers will not spot his connection as being illegal. By erasing relevant information he is able to alter local records as well such that the original owner of the device, should he get into repossessing it, will initially not be aware of the illegal access (however, once he receives his itemized bill he will discover what happened, but then it will be too late).

Targets of Attack: Services and Operating System

- analysis of operating system, security configuration
- manipulation of registry
- introducing viruses etc.

Target of Attack: Infrastructure

- manipulation of the terminal device: illegal use will not be detected immediately
- destruction of the device
- duplication and deployment of alien devices: feigning legal access.

These are the further risk potentials specific to mobile phones:

Hardware

The most primitive action is obviously the simple destruction or elimination of the device. Normally this does not present any strategic advantage concerning just a single device. The only benefit by such an action would be to wipe out traces. Otherwise it would not make sense. Much more profitable would be a purposeful hardware manipulation. This could be:

- deleting of information stored locally
- manipulation of locally kept data (changing contents)
- manipulation of applications (uninstalling, introducing malware)
- setting up a back door for later access to connected systems.

Device Characteristics

Generally speaking, spying on and manipulating device characteristics is a follow up on hardware attacks. Additional dangers result from:

- exchanging the real device against a dummy with identical characteristics, to be able at a later stage to pass authentication. After this all already mentioned possibilities continue to exist.
- Introducing additional storage media, to record the usage. By this a usage profile can be deduced, which could be of interest for various reasons for the spy, but also to uncover additional passwords for external applications. For such an operation to be successful the perpetrator has to come back and arrange for another theft to harvest the additional information or to revert the swap. This could really only be possible, if there are systematic security loopholes or completely careless handling.

Infection

Infection means the introduction of malware in its various forms (viruses, worms, Trojan horses). By being in possession of the device the classical venue to circumvent a firewall or a virus scanner within a communication network is no longer required. The attacker is able to implant his vermin in all tranquillity. With the next WLAN access or the next message to an email account it reaches the organisations network and can start to proliferate.

4.6.2.2 Attacker Does Not Possess the Device

This is a situation more difficult for the attacker. But a technically versatile attacker can still wreck havoc employing other means to get access to central applications with the help of an alien device. In this context here once again a summary of the equivalent risk analysis for PDAs:

Target of Attack: Applications

- spying on data
- manipulation of data including deletion
- gathering information about company processes
- analysis of operating system, security parameters
- manipulation of registry
- introducing viruses etc.

Targets of Attack: Services and Operating System

- hacking of authentication: by eavesdropping on the radio traffic getting hold of the authentication codes
- using creeping in methods to get into sessions; then
- operating system analysis, uncovering of security parameters
- manipulation of registry
- introducing viruses etc.
- denial of service: creating massive load on servers that are used for routing messages thus bringing the whole system to a standstill – in other contexts a favourite method to block Internet pages.

And these are the additional risk potentials for mobile phones:

By acoustic and electronic eavesdropping an attacker may gather important essential information for getting into the operating system and uncovering vital configuration data. These are, for example:

- authentication parameters
- access codes for applications
- man-in-the-middle attacks to join in in applications without being uncovered

Thereafter by employing certain services further channels open up to create further damage:

Target of Attack: Communication

- spoofing: all methods to obtain authentication codes, network protocols, system addresses
- man-in-the-middle camouflage: to sneak between two communicating partners without being noticed and thus obtain all important information necessary to gain access and successively spying
- protocol attack: changing protocols and mappings to render systems unusable
- eavesdropping, sniffing.

Target of Attack: Infrastructure

- theft of the terminal device
- eavesdropping on data traffic for later inference regarding the infrastructure itself.

Further risk potentials specific to mobile phones:

- DoS:

Similar as with the Internet mobile phone services are prone to the possibilities of Denial-of-Service situations, which can be provoked by flooding a device with data packets or buffer overflows such that a continued usage of the device becomes impossible. Communication has to be interrupted and re-started, which inevitably leads to data loss.

- Communication:

One has to distinguish between passive and active activities. Passive ones are:

- eavesdropping
- sniffing.

The possibilities in connection with eavesdropping have already been discussed. Concerning sniffing one has to distinguish between legal and agreed deployment of a network sniffer for analysis of a LAN or a WLAN against its illegal use. The latter is of interest here. Passive sniffers cannot be traced in the log files of the systems under attack. The following can be intercepted:

- information about access points
- data traffic
- authentication codes.

Sniffers are a favorite tool of war drivers.

The active variants include:

- DoS
- man-in-the-middle
- spoofing.

Since mobile phones can also connect to the Internet, spoofing is a relevant threat. Spoofing means pretending a faked identity, for example, a webpage supposed to be trustworthy – for example the homepage of a bank. The attacker will try to gather information about the bank account of the user by posing clever questions.

- Infrastructure:

The only possibilities to influence the infrastructure of a communication network without being in the possession of a legal device are to create disruptions of important communication processes by using one of the already mentioned methods. By gaining information about access codes and sneaking into sessions the attacker has all other possibilities to influence network security and availability.

4.6.3 General Precautionary Measures

4.6.3.1 Data

This is the first rule: store only what is absolutely necessary. Many data stored and carried around on mobile devices are only of use in the office, where they are stored on other media anyway. The more information is carried to the outside the higher the possibility that unauthorized persons get knowledge about this and may destroy or manipulate them.

4.6.3.2 Data Encryption

If it is really necessary to transmit sensitive data via public WLANs or comparable protocols, such data should be encrypted.

If possible, business (and private) email queries via mobile phone should be done via SSL (Secure Sockets Layer) connections. In this case it is verified, whether a security certificate has been deposited on the message server.

4.6.3.3 Firewalls

Even for mobile phones possibilities exist to implement firewalls. Other protection methods employ the Bluetooth protocol (not to be discussed further here).

4.6.3.4 Encryption on the Device

If possible, locally stored data should be encrypted as well.

4.6.3.5 Backup

Critical information should be saved on a separate device or medium. This claim has been put forward since the early days of IT, but is still not standard behavior. Because the probabilities for theft and loss are exceedingly higher in this context than those concerning traditional configurations, this demand is more important than ever. Even after theft organizations have to be able to continue to work normally.

4.6.3.6 The e-commerce Risk

Possibilities offered by the Internet or the usage of i-mode or WAP open up completely new risk potentials. These are similar to those mentioned earlier in connection with Internet banking: an attacker could use technical means to spy on bank data und misuse them later. Nothing at all should go without encryption.

4.7 SPECIAL CASE BLACKBERRIES

The manufacturers of Blackberries concede that they do not provide additional security features other than those already discussed for PDAs and above the usual standard concerning SMS and MMS traffic. SMS and MMS are not encrypted on BlackBerries. The manufacturers propose a number of other measures to increase security. These comprise:

- a special policy in organizations regulating external connection with BlackBerries. This is a typical task for a directive appropriate for all kinds of handhelds.
- "confirm on send": requesting the user to confirm that he really wants to transmit the message before actually sending it
- neutralize the forwarding function (prevents the dissimulation of malware)
- neutralize the possibility to communicate via non-encrypted messages between users without passing through a secure server.

There are additional possibilities to eliminate non-secure messages from BlackBerries by routing them only through a suitable BlackBerry server environment. In this way there exist the following configuration options:

- PIN messaging off
- SMS messaging off
- MMS messaging off.

This of course will take away some of the fun from the game, but excludes important security potentials at the same time.

Another possibility is the deployment of S/MIME [89] technology for emails. This technology is based on a general security philosophy relevant for any kind of communication and is not restricted to wireless networks only. Therefore it will not be discussed any further in detail here. S/MIME packages are on offer by the BlackBerry manufacturers and can be acquired separately. S/MIME supports among others:

- certificate validation
- cipher key synchronization
- encryption
- support of Smart Cards [90].

4.8 SMART PHONES

Smart Phones [91] represent an enhancement with respect to regular mobile phones (Fig. 4.9), having lead to a comprehensive integration of mobile phone services and PDA functionality:

Fig. 4.9 Smart Phone

At least the following services and functions will be found on them:

- GSM
- UTMS
- GPRS
- HSCSD
- WLAN

as protocols, and

- SMS, MMS
- emails
- Internet access

for communication. On top of this additional applications may be included, such as:

- GPS
- Office Software
- MP3 player
- digital cameras etc.

A special type of Smart Phone is the iPhone of Apple. Conclusions about security aspects concerning iPhones are also valid for other Smart Phones.

4.8.1 iPhone

iPhone is a product of Apple Computers (Figure 4.10):

Besides the classical telephone functions its main attractiveness is to be found in its support of all sorts of media services, especially as a sort of enhanced iPod for videos and music. Its operating system is a modification of MAC OS X. Its main applications contain:

- web browser
- email program
- calendar
- map service
- note pad
- YouTube player
- pocket calculator
- weather forecast service
- stock exchange service.

iPhones possess high data storage capacities and possibilities to connect to central applications via WLAN. This combination and the fact that iPhone users generally have a high tendency to down load all sorts of propositions creates unusual security

Fig. 4.10   iPhone

risks. Also, shortly after launch security loopholes were detected, which enabled attackers to crack critical passwords carrying root capabilities in a relatively easy way. These loopholes may have been closed as of now. But there still exits the possibility to connect to central applications via the Internet.

If an organization wants to use iPhones for remote access to its applications, it has to be aware that

- they possibly facilitate access to confidential data and
- they could be used as a transport device for malware.

The same is true for Smart Phones in general.

4.8.2 VoIP

Voice over IP [92] (VoIP) facilitates telephony using the Internet. By this technology classical telephone infrastructure can be avoided. Various terminal devices can be employed to this end. After the development of Smart Phones the same possibilities now exist for the mobile phone sector. For this purpose Smart Phones utilize the WLAN protocol to gain access to the Internet via its access points.

4.8.2.1 Additional Security Aspects Concerning VoIP

The more important ones are:
- Spoofing (Sec. 4.6.2)
- DoS (Sec. 4.6.2)
- SPIT (SPAM over Internet Telephony) [93]
- Vishing (faking false hotlines to obtain confidential user data).

4.9 SECURITY CHECK

The most serious dangers for security mostly occur in locations outside of an organization, when the user is traveling:
- in public transport
- in hotels
- in the premises of business partners.

Because of time pressure, overwork and reduced concentration chances rise that a device gets lost or stolen. But even within the buildings of an organization there are certain risks. To face the overall security potential a regular risk analysis at fixed time intervals should be carried out. For this purpose Table 4.2 maybe helpful:

Table 4.2 Risk Analysis

Question/Starting Position	Weight
Some employees work remotely from headquarters.	
Many employees travel regularly and need remote access to electronic communication media.	
Many employees need mobile phones to accomplish their work.	
Many employees possess company mobile phones.	
There is no clear policy concerning qualification for company mobile phones.	
There is no clear accountability for the distribution of mobile phones.	
There are no explicit rules regarding cost accountability for mobile phones.	
Against effective directives users still connect to central systems.	
End users create and download confidential data.	
Company culture as a whole is not very restrictive.	

The above table should be completed from the heads of departments or groups in a company. The result of the analysis of these entries gives a qualitative overall picture of the actual threat potential within an organization.

Weights may be assigned as usual:

- 1 for totally untrue
- 2 for probably untrue
- 3 maybe
- 4 probably true
- 5 absolutely true.

The results should be collected and evaluated by the security organism in the company. Departments obtaining a high hit rate should attract special attention. In certain cases measures should be taken to reduce the evaluated risk. To maintain sustainability such an audit should be carried out on a regular basis.

4.10 DIRECTIVE

The directive proposed in the section about PDAs can be applied analogously to other mobile telephones.

Directive for the Usage of Mobile Phones

The company provides mobile phones for a limited number of users. To obtain a user license a special application has to be filed (mobile phone application form). After assessment a license may be granted.

In special cases superiors may apply for mobile phones for their staff members. This is possible, if compelling business requirements can justify this. The application can be filed informally to the IT security officer.

The management of the communications department is responsible for the selection of compatible mobile phones and for organizing their support. Decisions concerning user authorization do not fall within its field of competence, which is also true for the provision of the necessary financial means for the procurement of individual devices. Costs for purchase and maintenance of mobile phone usage have to be borne by the different departments themselves.

Mobile phones, which belong to the company, may only be used for purposes in connection with the company's business. Any personal usage is excluded. Expenses that occur through personal usage by the user have to be borne by the user himself. Expenses that occur for the company through such personal usage will be billed by the company to the user.

It is prohibited to install unauthorized software on company mobile phones. It is equally prohibited to download additional software or services (like ring tones for example) on mobile phones.

It is forbidden to dock non-authorized mobile phones onto other company devices such as computers, laptops, servers or networks, to connect with them or synchronize with them without prior written permission.

Employees, who obtain a usage license, are responsible for the security of these devices. The devices have to be carried along permanently throughout a business trip. Stolen or lost mobile phones will have to be replaced by the user. The devices remain property of the company.

Sensitive and confidential information may not be stored on mobile phones. In case of loss or theft the IT security officer has to be informed without delay to trigger the necessary steps for remote deletion of contact, calendar and configuration data.

Non-compliance

Any non-compliance incident against this directive has to be notified to the IT security officer. Non-compliance may lead to disciplinary actions up to the dissolution of the employment contract. This is independent from other legal actions.

Acknowledgement of the Instruction

This directive should be part of comprehensive employee security instructions. At the end the following agreement can be signed:

Acknowledgement of the Mobile Phone Directive

"Please read the present mobile phone directive and countersign it at the bottom of the document. One copy with your signature will be kept by the IT security officer.

With your signature you acknowledge:

1. I have received the mobile phone directive, understood its meaning and agree with it.
2. I confirm that I will use mobile phones handed out to me by my employer exclusively for the company's business activities.
3. I agree that I shall carry all costs, which may occur for the company as a consequence of my private use.
4. I will not connect mobile phones to computers, laptops, servers, systems or networks, which have not been cleared for this.

5. I will not store confidential and security relevant data on mobile phones.

6. I understand that I am responsible for the security and replacement of the device after loss. The device remains the property of the company.

7. I understand that non-compliance regarding this directive can induce legal consequences.

> Name
>
> Signature
>
> Department
>
> Date"

It is the same as with PDAs: a directive (with or without signature) has only limited power to prevent havoc. Important is the general attitude of all parties concerned and the necessary discipline.

4.11 CHECKLIST

Table 4.3 summarizes all critical checks for the deployment of mobile phones.

Table 4.3 Checklist Mobile Phones

Does A WLAN already exist in your work environment?	When operating a wireless network additional security requirements have to be observed with respect to a cabled LAN.
Do you want to build a new WLAN?	In major organizations a WLAN should be part of the overall IT strategy including IT security strategy.
Are the responsibilities for security clearly regulated (strategically, organizationally, technically)?	The organizational security procedures comprise general organizational measures, technical measures concerning IT security, technical measures regarding communications.
	Unresolved responsibilities endanger regular operations.
Do the security guidelines contain a catalogue of countermeasures in case of security incidents?	Depending on the type of incident different countermeasures take effect.

Table 4.3 Contd. ...

	A classification of countermeasures is necessary.
Has the usage of mobile phones been regulated?	Besides the already existing security risks in WLANs mobile phones constitute completely new types of risks.
	High mobility and additional communication potentials increase potential security risks significantly.
Is a general security check intended for mobile phones?	To confront the overall risk, potential risk analyses should be carried out on a regular basis.
	A security check documents the distribution and usage of mobile terminals in an organization.
Are private mobile phones in use?	For reasons of cost savings or for freelancers private phones will be admitted occasionally.
	When these phones can be used for private purposes control mechanisms will fail.
Are company-owned mobile phones being deployed?	Generally companies provide their own mobile phones to their employees.
Are mobile phones only used for voice traffic?	Voice is the normal mode of mobile phone usage.
Are mobile phones used to transmit data as well?	There are various possibilities to transfer data by mobile phones.
Are mobile phones used in WLANs?	Specially equipped mobile phones permit a connection to WLANs (standard upgrade HSDPA).
	When transmitting confidential data special security precautions must be respected.
Are mobile phones used for the company's business outside the organization?	Normally mobile phones will be used outside the company.
	The use should be regulated on the basis of directives.
Are remote accesses to central applications frequently necessary?	Mobile employees need remote access.
	A separate security concept should be developed for regular remote accesses to applications.
Do many employees work with mobile phones from outside?	In some departments (field service, external assembly) all employees are equipped with mobile phones.

Table 4.3 Contd. ...

	A separate security concept should be developed for regular remote accesses to applications.
Has the deployment of mobile phones outside the organisation been regulated restrictively?	The usage should be regulated through appropriate directives.
	Usage of company mobile phones should not be left to the discretion of the user.
Is the usage of mobile phone permitted in hotels?	Hotels represent "unsecure areas" concerning communication security.
	Protective attitudes against eavesdropping are important..
Are mobile phones used on the premises of business partners?	The premises of business partners are "unsecure areas" concerning communication security.
	Protective attitudes against eavesdropping are important.
Have security directives regarding WLAN usage been documented?	Security directives constitute a separate area of a companies IT security strategy.
	Security aspects with regard to WLANs should be documented separately.
Are rules regarding the distribution and authorization for mobile phones in place?	Such rules should be part of directives.
	Non-existing rules will lead to uncontrolled growth.
Have selection criteria been defined for the purchase of these terminals?	A catalogue of criteria is useful to sound the market. Special attention should be given to security aspects.
	The purchase department should receive guidelines with appropriate criteria.
Are authentication procedures employed?	Authentication procedures are the main prerequisite for WLAN security.
	Without authentication procedures no WLAN should be operated.
Are applications protected by password?	Individual applications can be protected by passwords.
	Protection by passwords are a matter of course.

Table 4.3 Contd. ...

Is a password change strategy in place?	The change strategy comprises the rate of change as well as the password format.
	Change strategy should not be left to the discretion of the users.
Has a password change cycle been defined?	For the change cycle a time schedule should be communicated. Change should take place either monthly or at most quarterly.
	Passwords should be supplied with an expiry date.
Are complex password structures required?	The security of passphrases depends strongly on their length and character combination.
	Simple passwords can be guessed by an attacker easily.
Do alert procedures exist in case of security incidents?	Every organization should have a suitable alert process in place.
	Without any alert process a timely intervention is not guaranteed.
Do control mechanisms exist concerning deployment und usage of private terminals in the company?	Usage of private terminals should be subject to mandatory control mechanisms.
	In exceptional cases private devices may go online under defined conditions.
Are terminal devices inventoried?	The IT security officer together with IT management is responsible for documenting the existing infrastructure.
Will synchronization programs and communication protocols be updated regularly?	These software components should be kept at the most recent technical level to warrant continued compatibility and support by the manufacturer.
Is logging analysis carried out regularly to control access?	An appropriate management platform permits user logging, authentication and analysis.
	Logfiles register also access attempts by non-authorized persons.
Is the infrastructure checked regularly?	This comprises physical inspection as well as checks on all relevant communication protocols and log files.
	Checking the records should follow a regular schedule.
Are operating systems and hardware being brought up to date on a regular basis?	Updates and upgrades provide the latest standards in security.

Table 4.3 Contd. ...

	Falling behind in software and hardware levels might endanger warranty.
Are counter measures against eavesdropping in place?	Only by an efficient combination of organizational and technical measures can the overall risk be reduced.
	Eavesdropping for some length of time may reveal even encrypted passwords and data.
Are itemized bills analyzed regularly?	Itemized bills uncover non-authorized usage.
	Itemized bills should be ordered as a matter of course and analyzed.
Is one and the same device in use by several users?	Some companies allow this mode of operation by changing users for cost reasons.
	Changing users complicates the enforcement of control mechanisms.
Are users provided with SIM cards only?	Some users could be equipped with a SIM card instead of a dedicated mobile phone.
	SIM cards could get lost more easily. Besides there is no control about the terminal device on which they will be installed.
Is a SIM card management system in place?	SIM cards should be inventoried.
	Only an inventory allows the correct allocation to a user.
Is GSM employed?	GSM is the most popular mobile phone standard.
Is UMTS employed?	UMTS provides additional functions with respect to GMS (MMS for example),
Do mobile phones access e-commerce applications?	By using different protocols (Internet, WLAN) e-commerce transactions can be executed.
	e-commerce transactions have to be protected against spying (encryption).
Do local applications run on mobile phones?	Office and other applications can be installed or activated.
	Local applications could present an additional source for viruses.
Do clearing procedures exist for applications on terminals?	Only software for company needs and certified for this purpose should be allowed to go on stream for mobile phones.
	Private applications should have no place on such devices.

Table 4.3 Contd. ...

Are business data stored locally?	Some applications required local data storage.
	Local business data should be kept to a minimum.
Are only absolutely necessary data kept?	Some applications required local data storage.
	Minimum and maximum of permitted data should be fixed centrally.
Are memory extensions permitted?	Memory extensions facilitate uploads of spread sheets and other data.
	Memory extensions facilitate also uploads of unwanted applications.
Are central data bases accessed?	It is possible to tap confidential information from central data bases by remote access.
	Remote access of central data bases has to be controlled by special security provisions (encryption).
Are regular backups carried out for local data?	Backups become important, once a device has been lost or stolen.
	Without backup lost information has to be reconstituted tediously by hand.
Are data encrypted?	Encryption of data and storage media is a basic part of security strategy.
	Non-encrypted data can be spied on without effort.
Is SMS traffic permitted?	Via SMS short messages (160 characters) can be transmitted.
	SMS messages should not contain confidential information.
Is EMS traffic permitted?	EMS facilitates the transmission of longer messages by stringing together several SMS.
	EMS messages should not contain confidential information.
Is MMS traffic permitted?	MMS can be used to distribute photos or videos.
	MMS messages may contain viruses in their appendices.
Is i-mode being deployed?	i-mode allows Internet access with mobile phones.
	Internet access should be protected separately.
Is WAP being deployed?	WAP abbreviates Wireless Application Protocol. This service allows the transmission of information from the Internet.

Table 4.3 Contd. ...

	Internet access should be protected separately.
Is Internet access via mobile phones permitted?	The possibilities concerning Internet usage should be regulated by directives.
	Internet access should be protected separately.
Is UMA technology being deployed?	UMA facilitates WLAN access via mobile phones.
	UMA technology integrates voice and WLAN.
Does the organization already integrate voice and WLAN?	Integration of voice and WLAN means integration of voice and data.
	The combination of voice and data presents extraordinary challenges concerning security measures.
Is VoIP for WLAN being deployed?	WLAN also facilitates the implementation of VoIP strategies.
	This will permit connections via Access Points or hotspots.
Have email functions been defined for handhelds?	Any account structures should be specified beforehand.
	Email traffic should be reduced to the necessary.
Are central applications protected by firewalls?	Firewalls are indispensable preconditions for the secure operation of any network.
	Without firewalls no communication system should go live.
Are the access paths to central systems protected by virus scanners?	Virus scanner should be standard.
	Without virus scanners no communication system should go live.
Are BlackBerries permitted for mobile phone services?	BlackBerries possess an independent security architecture.
Have rules been developed for the employment of BlackBerries?	Their usage should be regulated by directives.
	BlackBerries require their own security provisions.
Is it possible to circumvent the server without encryption?	There is a theoretical possibility to transmit non-encrypted messages.
	Transmission of non-encrypted messages should be prevented.

Table 4.3 Contd. ...

Is the option "confirm on send" activated?	This feature requires an additional confirmation to prevent accidental transmission of non-encrypted or confidential information to the wrong addressee.
	The option "confirm on send" should be used if possible.
Has the forwarding option been deactivated?	Deactivation of the forwarding option prevents the proliferation of viruses.
	Deactivation of forwarding should be considered if useful in certain cases.
Has the function "PIN messaging" been de-activated?	PIN messaging facilitates message traffic to bypass the BlackBerry Enterprise Server.
	PIN messaging should be set to "off".
Has SMS been deactivated?	For BlackBerries SMS functions can be switched off.
	Deactivation of SMS should be considered if useful in certain cases.
Has MMS been deactivated?	For BlackBerries MMS functions can be switched off.
	Deactivation of MMS should be considered if useful in certain cases.
Has S/MIME been deployed?	S/MIME is a security package that provides additional encryption protection.
	For highly sensitive applications this additional investment should be considered.
Are Smart Phone permitted?	Smart Phones are enhancements of regular mobile phones having lead to the integration of comprehensive mobile phone services und PDA functionalities.
	The security of Smart Phones as terminal devices for central applications is questionable.
Are iPhones permitted?	iPhone is a product of Apple Corporation. Besides the classical telephone functions its main attractiveness lies in its support for media services.
	The security of iPhones as terminal devices for central applications is questionable.
Is the use of the digital camera permitted?	Many mobile phones have a digital camera integrated.

Table 4.3 Contd. ...

	The digital camera should only be used when documenting company specific information.
Are MP3 players permitted?	Many mobile phones have MP3 players integrated.
	MP3 functions facilitate the download of files which may contain viruses.

5

Bluetooth

5.1 INTRODUCTION

In the preceding chapters the basics and the security aspects in the wireless domain were entirely related to WLAN standards. Although the WLAN is the most important standard in this context, it is by no means the only one in wireless communication. In the following a communication standard for small distances will be introduced: Bluetooth.

Initially the technical basics such as protocols and system topologies will be dealt with. Then procedures concerning implementation and configuration will be discussed. After this the security aspects come into play. These security aspects deal with existing security features, risk potentials and possible countermeasures. In the end current developments and the future of this technology will be touched upon.

5.2 TECHNICAL BASICS

The technical basics of Bluetooth [94] comprise:

- protocols and
- system topologies.

Protocols are subject to continued review as is the case with all other protocols in wireless context in general. Its development will be traced back in the following section. Network construction thus depends on the state of these advancements.

5.2.1   Protocols

In the year 1998 the Bluetooth Special Interest Group (SIG) was founded with the intention to develop an authoritative communication standard for very short distances. One year later the standard 1.0a was proposed, and already at the end of that year version 1.0b was published (the features of the relevant versions will be discussed later on). In the beginning of 2001 version 1.1 was introduced as the first usable market standard. Meanwhile Bluetooth 2.1+DER (Enhanced Data Rate) [95] has arrived. However, the majority of the devices deployed is still working on the basis of version 1.2 released in 2003, whereas version 2.0 has only started to gain market and user share.

5.2.1.1   Structure

Figure 5.1 shows the structure of the Bluetooth protocol [96].

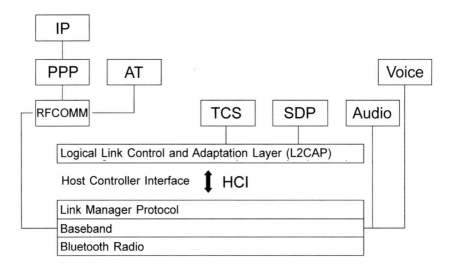

Fig. 5.1   Bluetooth Protocol

Besides the usual communication elements special attention should be given to the Link Manager Protocol (LMP) featuring the security checks. The remaining abbreviation stand for:

- RFCOMM: emulation of a serial interface
- AT: commanding mobile devices such as headsets
- SDP: Service Discovery Protocol
- TCS: Telephony Control Protocol Specification.

5.2.1.2 *Common Protocols and Performance*

Table 5.1 shows the Bluetooth versions together with their capability characteristics.

Table 5.1 Bluetooth Versions

Version	*Transmission Rate*
1.0	732.2 KBit/s
1.1	732.2 KBit/s
1.2	732.2 KBit/s
2.0 + DER	2.1 MBit/s
2.1 + DER	2.1 MBit/s

In addition to these characteristics one distinguishes three performance classes (Table 5.2).

Table 5.2 Bluetooth Performance Classes

Class	*Power in mW*	*Range in m*
1	100	100
2	2.5	10
3	1	1

5.2.1.3 *Features*

Bluetooth protocols are suited for data transmission over short distances for:

- mobile phones
- mouse
- laptops
- PDAs
- printer

- digital cameras
- video cameras
- web pads
- loudspeakers
- television sets
- earphones
- hands-free kits
- other similar devices.

(Meanwhile Bluetooth has entered the entertainment and toy realm; however, these applications will not be followed up here.)

A special feature is the possibility to define certain usage profiles [97] for data exchange. These profiles relate to the communicating devices to be employed. Table 5.3 lists a selection of such profiles.

Table 5.3 Bluetooth Profiles

Abbreviation	Designation	Meaning
GAP	Generic Access Profile	Basic Profile
RS-232	Serial Port Profile	Virtual Serial Interface
HSP	Head Set Profile	Hands-free Kit
HID	Human Interface Device Profile	Connection of Keyboards, Mouse etc.
DUN	Dial-up Network Profile	Telephone Dial-up by Computer
FTP	File Transfer Profile	File Transmission

5.2.2   System Topology

Bluetooth uses a frequency range between 2400 and 2480 MHz. On top of this a radio connection to fixed line telephony is possible. Altogether two different data channels are provided:

- Synchronous Connection Oriented (SCO) for voice
- Asynchronous Connectionless Link (ACL) for all other types of data.

5.2.2.1   Topology

The network, within which Bluetooth devices communicate, is called a Piconet. Such a Piconet [98] is assembled by the participating devices themselves. The number of devices that can be assembled in such a network amounts theoretically to 255. However of those only eight can be active at any given time. To function one device has to be designated as master. The other seven are called slaves. One and the same Bluetooth device can also be connected to several different Piconets at the same time – as long as it does occupy the master role (Figs. 5.2 and 5.3).

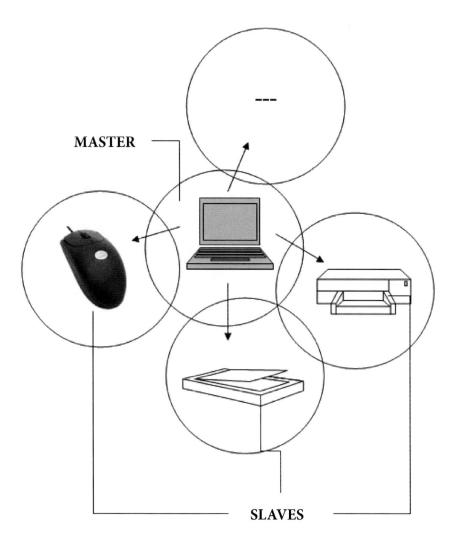

Fig. 5.2 Piconet

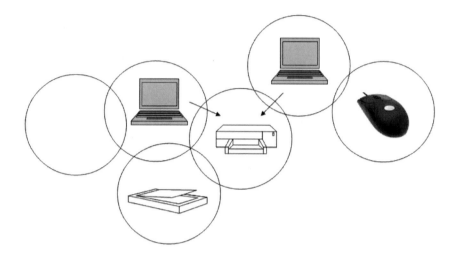

Fig. 5.3 Piconet Overlap

5.2.2.2 Connection Set-up

Every Bluetooth device has a Device Address with a length of 48 bits. A Bluetooth device continually polls its environment (Inquiry) to find out whether another Bluetooth device is within its reach and wants to communicate. Once devices have been recognized a paging request is initialized to set up a distinctive connection. The paging device then functions as master and discloses its address. Within a Piconet point-to-point connections as well as 1-to-n connections can be initialized.

5.3 CONFIGURATION

5.3.1 Options

The options discussed under the subject of configuration comprise basically:

- management of the device pool
- configuration as such concerning a single device
- administration of device characteristics

- searching for devices within a network
- admission of a device to a network.

5.3.2   Configuration

5.3.2.1   *Adding a Device*

The following example is based upon a workflow under Windows XP (it only functions after the necessary patch with the Bluetooth options has been installed):

- click Start
- click "execute"
- enter "bthprops.cpl"
- OK
- screen with "Bluetooth Options" opens up
- select "Add"
- activate check box "Device is set up and can be recognized"
- continue
- select device
- continue
- enter master key of the device (the security provisions will be discussed in detail further down)

If for example a printer should be added the following steps have to be executed (precondition is the existence of a Bluetooth adapter on the PC):

- startmenu
- printers and fax
- add printer
- continue
- select "Bluetooth" printer
- continue
- follow the instructions that have been delivered with the printer.

5.3.2.2 Device Characteristics

The device characteristics concern mainly those necessary for communicating within the network. These comprise:

- device type
- address of the Bluetooth adapter
- date and time of the last connection
- use of the master key
- type of service supported by the device
- possibility to change the device designation.

5.3.3 Connecting to the Network

Bluetooth device possesses a device address of 48-bit length (BDA: Bluetooth Device Address). Connection can only take place once the device is active (Fig. 5.4). If this is the case the device address is broadcast every two seconds. At the same time the device is searching for other devices within its transmission range every 5.6 seconds (Inquiry). For this to happen the search function has to be activated at the device. The initiating device will be master after successful connection.

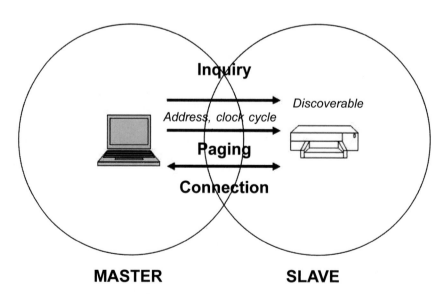

Fig. 5.4   Connection Set-up

The master device then sends per "Paging" its address and its timing cycle to the slave(s). Only after this the connection process will be completed.

5.4 SECURITY ASPECTS

As is the case with other communication protocols Bluetooth is also prone to attacks from outside. These risks are in part identical to those known for WLANs, partially specific, because they are related to Bluetooth technology. In the following those security mechanisms provided by Bluetooth as a standard will be presented first. Thereafter the general and specific risk potentials will be identified before discussing the appropriate countermeasures to neutralize such risks.

5.4.1 Instruments

Bluetooth uses various system-specific security relevant adjustments and possibilities. These contain:

- security operations modes
- cryptographic mechanisms
- authentication
- encryption

5.4.1.1 Security Operations Modes [99]

Bluetooth provides different operations modes. They stand for different levels of security. These are effectively:

- Mode 1 (non-secure): no special security provisions, no authentication required
- Mode 2 (Service Level Security): security mechanisms at the service level
- Mode 3 (Link Level Security): security mechanisms at the link level – cryptographically (authentication) and/or data encryption.

5.4.1.2 *Cryptographic Mechanisms*

The basis for the cryptographic method is link cipher keys in connection with the so-called pairing method [100] between two devices. This cipher key (length: 128 bits) constitutes itself from a combination of the device addresses and a random number for each device. The generated random numbers will be transferred to the other device respectively. To render this transfer secure an initialization cipher key is required constituted from the following elements (Fig. 5.5):

- another random number
- address of one of the involved devices
- PIN.

The PIN has to be identical for both devices (length: up to 16 Bytes).

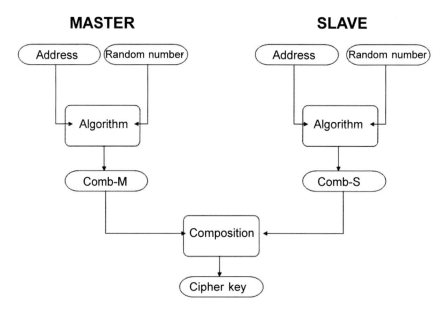

Fig. 5.5   Key Construction

5.4.1.3 *Authentication*

Authentication works (initialized from one side) from device to device (point-to-point). The following automatism will be executed (Fig. 5.6):

- Authentifier sends random number to authenticator.
- Authenticator calculates a reply from the random number, the combination cipher key and its own address (32 bits).
- Authenticator sends reply to authentifier.
- Authentifier executes the identical calculation. If both results are found to match, the desired link will be established.

Authentificator   **Authenticator**

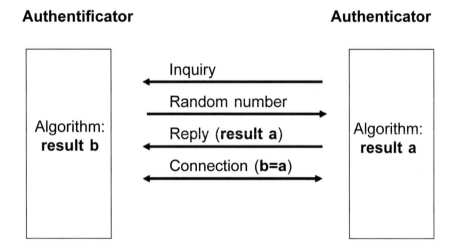

Fig. 5.6 Authentication

5.4.1.4 *Encryption*

Encryption (Fig. 5.7) can only take place after authentication and establishment of a stable link. For this to happen another cipher key has to be agreed upon. It is constituted from:

- the combination cipher key
- an offset and
- a random number.

For encryption two modes of operations are offered:

- point-to-point or
- point to multi-point master to several slaves in the Piconet).

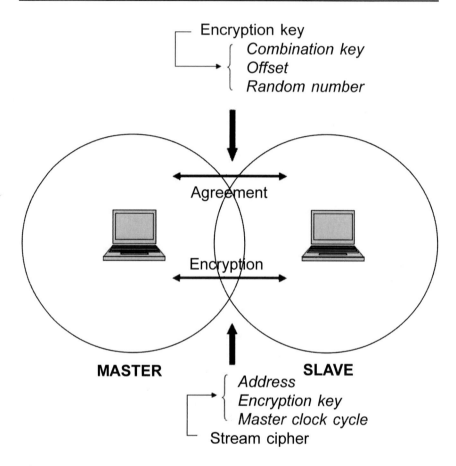

Fig. 5.7 Encryption

Encryption is provided for data transfer only by using a stream cipher made of:

- device address
- encryption cipher key
- timing cycle of the master.

Encryption on the terminal devices has to be done separately.

5.4.2 Risk Potentials

The security risks in connection with Bluetooth traffic, the terminal devices and applications in question is partially similar to those known for WLANs and mobile phone usage. In addition there are specific sources of endangerment brought about by Bluetooth operations and its own security mechanisms themselves. The following lists the most important problem areas:

- man in the middle attacks:

Someone sneaks in between two communicating devices. This is facilitated if no data encryption is used.

- PINs:

The main challenge is to employ PINs that cannot be guessed easily.

- Tracking:

Once the devices are switched on and running "Inquiry" they can be detected easily because of the polling process.

- DoS attack:

By intense transmission of unsolicited information to one and the same address a device can be blocked.

- Spying of data on terminal devices:

After successful spying local data can be read, manipulated or deleted.

- Modification of the configuration:

There is special hacking software available able to access configurations and change parameters.

- Bugs in the Bluetooth software:

Known bugs enable non-authorized access by attackers.

- Default settings:

Devices are delivered with default settings. These should be changed immediately after acquisition.

- Long and frequent connections using the same key:

Continually sending connection cipher keys and long standing connections themselves facilitate the decryption of that key by determined attackers. The pattern of these connections constitutes such an opportunity for an attacker.

- Weak spots concerning the encryption algorithm:

As any other algorithm Bluetooth also has certain weak spots providing versatile attackers with possibilities to enter into communication.

- Risk of theft:

Because these are mobile devices the risk of theft is higher.

- No password protection at the device level:

In case of missing passwords stolen devices can be utilized by attackers directly.

- Malware:

As for any other network Picontes are targets for viruses, Trojan horses and relatives.

5.4.3 Countermeasures

The following countermeasures improve the security of Bluetooth applications:

- Procurement criteria

There exist certain criteria, which need to be respected when purchasing Bluetooth devices. They comprise:

- minimal length of cipher keys
- possibilities to change default settings
- additional security software on offer by the manufacturer

- Default settings

All delivered default settings should be changed prior to the first deployment of any device.

- Services

All services delivered but not to be used should be deactivated or uninstalled.

- Transmission power

To reduce tracking risks the transmission power should be kept to a minimum.

- Security mode

Security mode should be set to 2 or 3. Security mode 1 is out of the question.

- Encryption

All communications should generally be encrypted. Care is to be taken that at a minimum all data relevant to connections are stored in encrypted fashion on the devices themselves. There should be a separate policy for data encryption.

- PIN

PINs should be composed out of all available character combinations (not only letters or numbers but also special characters in upper and lower case variations). The maximum length offered by the manufacturer should be fully used.

- Tracking

It is difficult to neutralize tracking altogether as long as the devices are active. By combining several measures, however, security can be enhanced:

- switching the device to "hidden"
- changing the device designation
- deactivating devices not currently in use.

- Firewalls

To protect against hacking software Bluetooth devices should be equipped with firewalls and other fences against viruses if technically feasible.

- Theft/loss

In case of theft all cipher keys relevant for linking should be deleted on all remaining devices.

- Authentication

Authentication procedures at device level should be installed if technically feasible.

- Access

If possible devices should be physically protected against unauthorized access.

5.5 THE FUTURE

The Bluetooth future points into two directions:

- Enhancement of the standard and
- opening up new areas of deployment.

5.5.1   Enhancement

These are some of the features to be expected in the future:

- support of additional high speed channels (Seattle Release)
- Enhancement of the protocol layer L2CAP
- ultra-broadband with up to 480 MBit/s
- additional deployment models concerning technologies (Profiles)
- equipping mobile devices with RFID [101] technology

5.5.2   New Areas of Deployment

The deployment of Bluetooth already surpasses the area of traditional information technology. Today applications can also be found in the entertainment sector. This shall not be followed up here. Of importance will be applications

- in car electronics
- in manufacturing control
- in machine and plant operations
- in intelligent machine communication.

These areas result in interfaces to other fields of business and therefore to central applications. In this case the already discussed security risks will again become relevant.

5.5.3   Bluetooth 4.0

Latest developments aim to bring Bluetooth 4.0 [102] to market. It will offer higher transmission rates for devices that use less power. Three options will be available:

- standard
- high speed
- low energy.

The low energy option is obligatory for anyone, who wants to build devices adhering to this standard. The high speed option cater for transmission rates of up to 54 MBit/s with a possible reach of 100 meters. Low energy operates in the 2.4 GHz frequency band. Its main applications are seen in the medical field.

5.6 CHECKLIST

Table 5.4 regroups all relevant security aspects with regard to Bluetooth applications.

Table 5.4 Checklist Bluetooth

Do you already deploy Bluetooth?	All Bluetooth applications in operation should be subject to regular security checks.
Is Bluetooth used in an organization?	Bluetooth applications in organizations should be subject of internal security strategies.
Are you using Bluetooth as a private person?	Even in private environments risks are basically comparable technically to those in larger organizations.
Are you planning to introduce a Bluetooth application?	When implementing Bluetooth for the first time some general security aspects have to be taken into account.
Are the responsibilities for security clearly regulated (strategically. organizationally, technically)?	The organizational security procedures comprise general organizational measures, technical measures concerning IT security, technical measures regarding communications.
	Unresolved responsibilities endanger regular operations.
Do the security guidelines contain a catalogue of countermeasures in case of security incidents?	Depending on the type of incident different countermeasures take effect.
	A classification of countermeasures should be obligatory.
Is the usage of Bluetooth subject to regulation?	Bluetooth applications should be taken into account by the internal security strategy.
	Unregulated usage left to the discretion of end users constitutes a serious risk potential.
Have security guidelines been documented regarding the usage of Bluetooth?	Bluetooth usage should be part of the organizational security concept.
	Users should be committed to the adherence to security standards.
Does an authorization concept exist for applications?	An authorization concept should be in place as part of user security as a matter of course.
	Without controlled access rights intruders will meet open doors.

Table 5.4 Contd. ...

Are applications protected by passwords?	Individual applications can be protected by passwords.
	Without passwords all applications can be accessed by anyone.
Is a password change strategy in place?	The change strategy comprises the rate of change as well as the password format.
	Change strategy should not be left to the discretion of the users.
Has the password change cycle been defined?	For the change cycle a time schedule should be communicated. Change should take place either monthly or at least quarterly.
	Passwords should be supplied with an expiry date.
Are complex password structures required?	The security of passphrases depends strongly on their length and character combination.
	Simple passwords can be guessed by an attacker easily.
Do alert procedures exist in case of security incidents?	Any organization should have a suitable alert process in place.
	Without any agreed upon alert process reactions will result in activism.
Are terminal devices inventoried?	The IT security officer together with IT management is responsible for documenting the existing infrastructure.
Is the infrastructure checked regularly?	This comprises physical inspection as well as checks on all relevant communication protocols and log files.
	Checking the records should follow a regular schedule.
Are configuration responsibilities sorted out?	Bluetooth adjustments can be done from basically any workstation.
	Restrictive measures have to be taken to allow configuration only be administrators.
Is security mode 1 in place?	Mode 1 does not use any special security mechanisms and no authentication procedures.
	Mode 1 should in no case be in operation.
Is security mode 2 in place?	This mode provides security mechanisms at the service level.
	Mode 2 should be the minimum standard.

Table 5.4 Contd. ...

Is security mode 3 in place?	This mode provides security procedures at the link level (encryption of messages and data).
Are cryptographical procedures used to authenticate access to the Piconet?	The basis of those cryptographical procedures are connection cipher keys in combination with a pairing mechanism between devices.
	Lacking authentication by Piconet subscribers will facilitate access by non-authorized third parties.
Are data encrypted?	Encryption can proceed only after authentication. For this special cipher keys have to be agreed upon.
	Not encrypted data can be easily spied upon.
Are data on local storage media encrypted?	Bluetooth security provisions end after the communication process.
	For encryption on local media the usual organizational standards should take effect.
Are complex PINs in use?	This constitutes a main problem, once PINs are used that can be guessed easily.
	Maximum PIN length should be used together with special characters.
Are devices switched on, even when they are not in use?	Devices should be switched off, when they are not in use.
	Once devices are switched on they can be localised easily because of the polling mechanism.
Are the standard security settings of the devices kept in place?	Standard settings should be changed immediately after purchase.
	Information about standard settings are publicly available.
Are frequent connections or connections of long duration using the same cipher key common practise?	Continual usage of the same cipher key facilitates the discovery of this key by determined attackers because of these connection patterns.
Are devices protected by passwords?	Devices can also be protected by passwords.
	Without password protection stolen devices can be used directly by attackers.
Have procurement criteria been defined for Bluetooth devices?	They should take into account the security relevant features of manufacturers.

Table 5.4 Contd. ...

	Those include: minimal length of cipher keys, change provisions of pre-adjustments and other special security software.
Are services not in use deactivated?	Services included in the delivery but not intended for use should be deactivated.
	Any service constitutes its own risk potential.
Is transmission power kept to a minimum?	There exists a compromise between desired and security relevant range.
	Because Bluetooth devices are continuously polling transmission power should be kept to the utmost minimum necessary.
Are provisions against tracking in place?	By combining certain measures security can be enhanced.
	These include: change of device designation and deactivation when out of use.
Is the device number changed?	The device number can be changed with the hep of the configuration software.
	By changing the device number tracking will be made more difficult.
Are Bluetooth devices protected by firewalls?	On Bluetooth devices firewalls can be installed.
	Firewalls are standard features of any security philosophy.
Does a master plan exist in case of theft?	After theft all connection cipher keys have to be deleted on the remaining devices.
	Mobile Bluetooth devices are especially prone to theft or loss.
Are devices physically protected against external access?	If possible devices should be protected by physical means against unauthorized access.
	Mobile Bluetooth devices are especially prone to theft or loss.

6

Infrared

6.1 BACKGROUND

Besides wireless applications based on WLAN and Bluetooth technologies communication via infrared radiation is on offer for some time. Infrared is light with wavelengths between 7.8×10^{-7} and 10^{-3} m corresponding to a frequency range of 3×10^{11} Hz up to 4×10^{14} Hz. One advantage of infrared radiation is its marginal harmfulness and susceptibility against electrical interference. One disadvantage is its small reach. Other advantages include:

- simple and low cost implementation
- low electrical power requirements
- directed point-to-point connection
- efficient and reliable data transmission.

For infrared communication standards have been developed which are oriented to possible applications. In the following these standards will be presented with regard to their architecture including transmission protocols. Thereafter possible applications will be considered and potential risks discussed. A small checklist at the end of this section lists key points to be observed when choosing and implementing infrared communication.

6.2 IRDA

Infrared has already been in use as transmission medium for some time for controllers, printers, pocket calculators and PDAs. In 1993 HP, IBM and Sharp initiated a group called Infrared Data Association (IrDA) [103] to promote the development of an industrial standard for infrared communication. Already in 1995 the first products adhering to this standard were launched on the market. They comprised:

- notebooks equipped with an infrared interface
- PDAs
- printers
- infrared adapters for PCs.
- Contrary to its predecessors, which used proprietary protocols, devices adhering to IrDA are capable to communicate between different applications on hardware from diverse manufacturers.

Table 6.1 contains different data rates corresponding to a reach of about 1 m in line of sight corresponding to the relevant IrDA protocol [104] specifications.

Table 6.1 IrDA Data Specifications

IrDA Data Specification	Transmission Rates [KBit/s]
SIR	9,6–115,2
MIR	576-1152
FIR	4000
VFIR	16 000
UFIR	96 000

6.2.1 General Considerations

Figure 6.1 shows a systematic comparison between classical wire bound against infrared connection [105]:

There are two decisive elements:

- the protocol handler and
- the optical transceiver (sending and receiving units).

Figure 6.2 shows the schematic interplay between a peripheral device – in this case a laptop – and the interface of another system:

From right to left the following items are visible:

- laptop
- optical transceiver

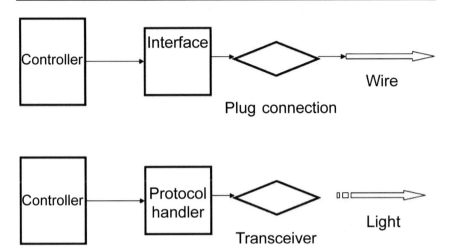

Fig. 6.1 Wire against Infrared

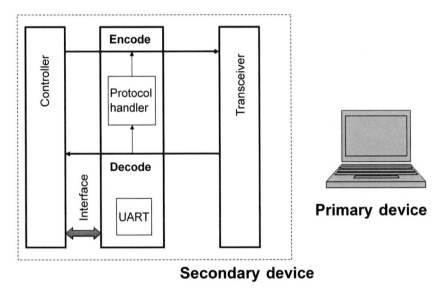

Fig. 6.2 Infrared Connection

- protocol driver
- host controller
- universal asynchronous sending and receiving units.

The most important layers of the protocol according to the OSI standard are:

- Physical Layer
- Link Layer
- Application Layer.

Link Management and Application Layer themselves have again substructures. In the following these protocols will be discussed in more detail. All layers are implemented in the protocol driver.

6.2.2 Protocol

The Physical Layer resides at the bottom (Fig. 6.3):

Asynchron Serial IR (SIR) 9600-115200 baud	Synchron Serial IR (SIR) 1, 15 Mbaud	Synchron Fast IR (FIR) 4 Mbaud

Fig. 6.3 Physical Layer

The Physical Layer fixes the data format. Up to three specifications from Table 6.1 can be implemented. Most devices such as PDAs employ SIR (Serial IR). PCs and some printers need FIR (Fast Serial IR).

The next layer is the Link Layer. This layer determines the connection type (Fig. 6.4):

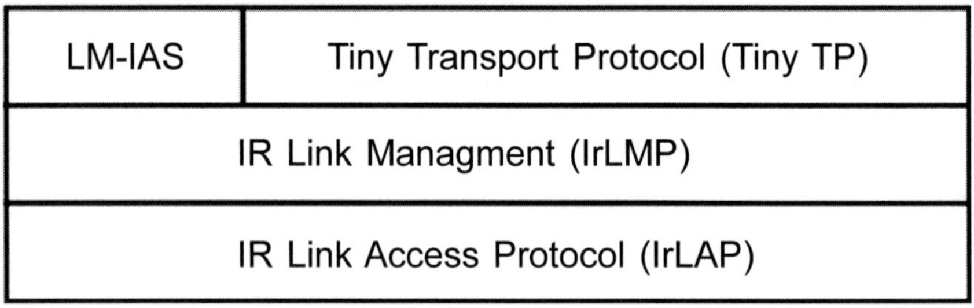

LM-IAS	Tiny Transport Protocol (Tiny TP)
IR Link Managment (IrLMP)	
IR Link Access Protocol (IrLAP)	

Fig. 6.4 Link Layer

The Link Layer is divided into sublayers:

- Link Access Protocol (IrLAP)
- Link Management (IrLM)
- optional transport protocols.

The layers provide for:

- data routing
- error corrections in data packages
- link management
- information structuring for the Application Layer

of the protocol stacks. On top of all resides the Application Layer (Fig. 6.5).

IrTRAN-P	IrObex	IrLAN	IrCOMM	IrMC

Fig. 6.5 Application Layer

This is where all the different application protocols reside. Here the factual object transmission (files, programs, photos etc.) is managed. The characteristics of these objects have to be defined beforehand.

IrCOMM stands for IrDA Standard Specification, which replaces the traditional serial and parallel interfaces.

6.3 APPLICATIONS

If IR communication shall be implemented for certain terminal devices technical requirements have to be checked and – if necessary – certain features to be installed. Implementation itself is relatively straight forward. Communication proceeds according to protocol (Sec. 6.3.3).

6.3.1 Terminal Devices

IrDa interfaces are available on:

- PDAs

- notebooks
- mobile phones
- printers
- pagers
- special watches, to measure heart beat for example.

6.3.2 Preconditions

To facilitate IrDa communication for notebooks, PCs or PDAs a digital interface is required as well as an analogue front end component. The latter can be connected via an RS-232 serial port for up to certain transmission rates (SIR) or via a USB adapter. Many devices on the market already have built-in infrared ports: laptops, PDAs, mobile phones. In addition the necessary driver software has to be found on the device.

6.3.3 Communication

Figure 6.6 shows the connecting sequence according to the standard IrDA protocol:

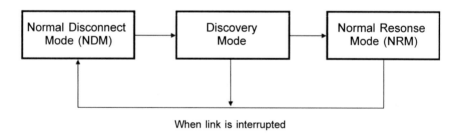

When link is interrupted

Fig. 6.6 Connection Sequence

Three modes are possible:
- normal disconnect mode
- discovery mode and
- normal response mode.

These modes shall be discussed now:

6.3.3.1 Normal Disconnect Mode

Figure 6.7 illustrates normal disconnect mode.

Primary device

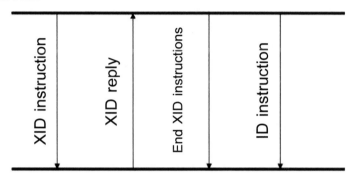

Secondary device

Fig. 6.7 Normal Disconnect Mode

NDM is the mode under which a device is polling for other IrDa standard devices. In this case the device sends XID (exchange identification) instructions within a time window of between 0 and 7 seconds. As soon as a second device is within reach of the first it will reply and reserve the time window. After this the second device will ignore all following XID messages. The IrDA protocol allows to distinguish between up to 8 different other devices. The first device emits a broadcast ID to which the other device does not respond.

6.3.3.2 Discovery Mode

Figure 6.8 illustrates discovery mode.

Under this mode the communicating devices negotiate their mutual parameters. The first device sends an SNRM (Set Normal Response Mode) instruction together with certain parameters and connection addresses. The other device sends a UA reply with parameters using the mentioned address. Thereafter the first device opens up a channel for IAS queries, which the second device then confirms. The features include:

- IR baud rate
- size of data packages
- delivery time and others.

Primary device

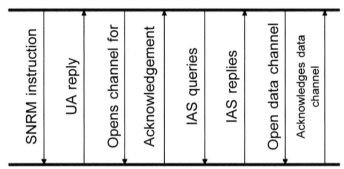

Secondary device

Fig. 6.8 Discovery Mode

These parameters are now being exchanged to find the highest common denominator to optimize performance. Now the first device has to come forward with the request for data. For a PDA this happens once the first data package for transmission is ready. For PCs a special program has to be installed to manage the IR port. The second device confirms that the channel is now open for data.

6.3.3.3 *Normal Response Mode*

Figure 6.9 illustrates normal response mode.

Normal response mode is the mode under which data and control information are sent to and fro. Status information is important to find out whether a connection is still active and not blocked. Should the connection be blocked because a time out has been reached the device is reset to the NDM state. As soon as communication is finished the first device disrupts the connection. The second device confirms this and both return to the NDM state.

Primary device

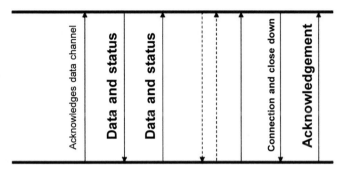

Secondary device

Fig. 6.9 Normal Response Mode

6.4 SECURITY ASPECTS

Security checking provided by the IrDA standard is only concerned with technical safeguarding at the protocol level such as transmission errors [106]. Authentication procedures, password protection and encryption are not provided at this level. This could theoretically mean that IR communication is weak against recording and eavesdropping. In this respect these are higher security risks in comparison with classical LAN applications. If at all, relevant security mechanisms would have to be introduced at the application level.

One consequence would be to avoid continuous operation of IR interfaces, since otherwise non-authorized persons could send data to a device using such an interface. For different devices there exist different risks:

- laptop: data and programs
- PDA: SMS, data and programs
- mobile phones: SMS.

All these pieces of information could theoretically be infected by malware.

An additional aspect concerning security can be regarded as positive and is due to the fact that IR communication has a short range and thus can only happen within a reduced area. There is, however, a residual risk emanating from radiation scattering of the communication components.

6.5 CHECKLIST

Table 6.2 Checklist IrDA

Check Item	Reply
Do you consider the deployment of infrared?	
Which types of devices will be chosen?	
Which applications are planned?	
Who are the users?	
Which transmission rate is under consideration?	
Will the devices be linked to other networks?	
Are the locations suited for infrared radiation?	
Are the locations protected against the detection of radiation scattering?	
Are the devices equipped with the necessary drivers?	
Are the devices equipped with the necessary infrared interfaces?	

7

Security Policy

In the preceding chapters two typical directives have been introduced (for PDAs and for mobile phones). The comprehensive directive proposed in this chapter contains some general elements, which can serve as the basis for any particular directive in an organization. For specific applications templates are presented, which have to be completed in the appropriate places. To do this contents from the preceding chapters in this book could be used.

7.1 INTRODUCTION

Wireless Security is part of a comprehensive concept regarding IT security. The latter can be divided into numerous documents all being mutually referred to each other and their complexity depending on the installation in question. It can be distinguished between strategic, technical and organizational measures and their corresponding directives. According to these levels the group of people concerned with these instructions varies as well. A directive for the design of firewalls is of no interest to the common user. He wants to know what the structure of his passwords should look like.

7.1.1 Security Requirements

Security requirements are visible on different levels of relevance:
- at the strategic level and its relation to the overall organization
- as tools to satisfy certain specifications

- through groups of people, who are responsible for specifications.

These different dimensions will be taken care of in the following. They are again related to specific risk estimates and possible countermeasures.

7.1.2 Risks

Risks again can be categorized multi-dimensionally:
- according to objects
- according to potential damage
- or as combination of both.

Additionally risks vary depending on the progress of attacks: the further an invader progresses in a system the higher will be the remaining risk. Risks can never be completely eliminated. Aim and subject of this directive is to minimize all possible risks one can think of. For those risk potential, which will follow later, and which are technology dependent, plausible risk scenarios will be developed together with relevant pre-emptive and compensational measures.

7.1.3 Measures

As explained further down one has to distinguish between two categories of measures:
- organizational and
- technical.

Both operate in concert and complement each other. Measures can be of general nature, which constitute a security environment and which generally controls security loopholes. These include directives, organizational structures and technical security installations at hardware and software level. Additionally quite a number of specific measures exist, which cover specific security risks and are relevant for specific cases. The relevant processes have to be implemented. Such measures will be discussed in detail.

7.2 SCOPE

The scope of IT security is limited by two criteria:

- organization
- time.

The scope concerning organization refers to the organizational units in a company, for which this system and its documentation are relevant. Normally all units are included. Exceptions may be outsourced units, subsidiaries or affiliated companies. In times of transition after fusion with other companies for example the possibility exists that certain departments, which may be using different IT systems, are controlled in a different fashion. These exceptions have to be documented properly.

Timely restriction of the scope refers to version levels. Every document has a version number referring to the main document. The validity statement refers to the actual version, exceptionally also to sections of past versions. In any case: the latest update is valid. This comprises statements as to how individual documents are processed. Changes are to be recorded in a version history up to the final release.

7.2.1 Normative References

The whole complex of subjects concerning IT security is again influenced by national standards and directives, some of which will be briefly mentioned. Detailed information can be obtained from the original documents:

7.2.1.1 Legal Regulations

Every country issues laws, which may also be pertinent to IT security under different aspects. These include:

- data privacy protection
- laws regulating information and communication services
- laws regulating telecommunications
- signature regulations
- and many others.

7.2.1.2   Guidelines and Standards

Government agencies offer guidelines based on international standards concerning IT security. Three of these standards will be outlined in the following:

7.2.1.3   Standard ISO/IEC 13335 [107]

This standard together with the two others presented here were developed in cooperation with the International Electrotechnical Commission in Geneva. This document outlines general principles as a reference base for more specific standards. It mainly contains:

- concepts and models for security in information and communication technology
- technical preconditions for the management of security risks
- guidelines concerning network security.

7.2.1.4   Standard ISO/IEC 17799 [108]

This standard offers approaches and step sequences for the strategic implementation of IT security systems. Detailed technical instructions are not included in this document. Its character is recommendatory without any binding force.

7.2.1.5   Standard 27001 [109]

The title of this standard reads: Information Technology – Security Techniques – Information Security Management Systems Requirements Specifications. This standard also has recommendatory character. Technical instructions for implementation are not given.

7.3   INFORMATION AND COMMUNICATION SECURITY

IT security plays a major role when systems are implemented. It can be regarded as a stand-alone subject or be part of IT quality management in general. Even if a separate IT quality organization exists, mutual interconnections and dependencies are so multiple that one cannot be considered without the other. IT quality management is a precondition for a clean implementation of security aspects. On the other hand, without taking security aspects into account there will be no sustainability in quality control.

Figure 7.1 shows the relationship between IT quality management and IT security in an overall project.

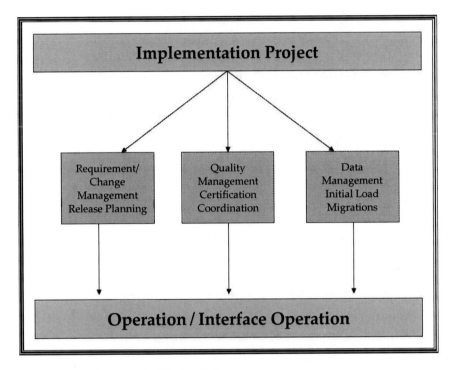

Fig. 7.1 IT Security In Project Management

The compliance of security requirements depends on the strategic placement of these tasks in a company as a whole. It will be outlined, which preconditions have to be initiated for this role. Important is the involvement of all project members at all times.

7.3.1 Strategic Involvement

IT security management is part of the overall security management covering the whole company – comprising all other material and immaterial goods as well as all employees. As such IT security management should be integrated methodically and process related into the overall concerns of security management. When talking about IT security management it is understood that the whole complex of IT and communication security is addressed.

IT security is achieved by a number of conceptual and organizational measures as well as the necessary technical preconditions, which are relevant to reach defined security objectives. These are the areas of concern:

- IT processes
- computer systems
- hardware
- software
- communication installations
- data
- documentation.

Security and Safety Engineering is the platform, on which technical preconditions for IT security can be created. The requirements can be derived from security criteria specific to a company, fixed by management after consulting with security experts. Among them are such classical criteria as

- data integrity
- confidentiality etc.

together with for example availability and authenticity. If a company deploys wireless communication networks, these criteria will look different from those for pure LAN applications. The principle has to be mutually agreed at the top level and communicated as binding security policy. Security policy should be positioned as part of the company's guiding principles, and should be furnished with the necessary competences at top management level.

On the basis of these definitions documents structured in hierarchical manner are drafted on the various execution levels, transforming these guiding principles into directives to be filled with life.

7.3.2 Security Organization

As a matter of course all employees and therefore all members of a project team have to be briefed about all valid security directives in a company. This may happen at the instant of providing an email account for example, and by then sending the relevant information. In special cases such as working with a WLAN the persons concerned should receive the necessary instructions separately. Instructing administrators should be obligatory in any case, since these persons have access to sensitive company data and configurations. Security aspects concerning administrators normally exceed those of common users.

After successful training, instruction and receiving the relevant security documentation every employee has to acknowledge by his signature on a special form that he has been informed, that he agrees with the directive and will respect it. The signed acknowledgement has to be archived by the IT security organization.

Table 7.1 recapitulates the strategic preconditions to constitute an IT security management.

Table 7.1 Checklist IT Security

Does an IT security management exist?	IT security management deals with all security aspects concerning implementation and operation of IT installations.
Have the concerns of IT security management been documented?	Precondition for an effective IT security management is the relevant documentation.
Are current IT standards taken into account with regard to security management?	ISO/IEC 13335, 17799, 27001
Have IT security criteria been documented?	Security is classified according to such criteria as confidentiality, availability, integrity etc.
Will the participants of IT security trainings acknowledge their participation by signature?	The participation in security trainings should be documented in the interest of all concerned.
Is the adherence to security directives monitored regularly?	The monitoring of the adherence to security directives should follow an appropriate action plan.

7.3.3 Approval Process

Organizational procedures have to be introduced to secure the approval of different services or objects, including:

- allocation of accounts
- access authorization to applications
- control over terminal devices.

Normally three instances are concerned with this process:

- applicant
- supervisor
- clearing officer.

The transaction has to be documented and downstream organizational units have to be informed (controlling, procurement etc.). Once the applicant leaves the organization all authorizations become invalid and have to be withdrawn.

7.3.4 Confidentiality

Another important transaction to improve the security of an organization is the commitment to confidentiality. Generally such a commitment is governed by the work contract such that no separate documents have to be drafted. Additionally these regulations are still valid for the time after a person has left an organization. However, occasionally the need arises for specific confidentiality instructions. This can be the case for example, when a person gets into contact with highly sensible data while working for a specific project. In such cases the confidentiality commitment may include restrictive information policies against units and persons internal to the organization. Sometimes the signature under an appropriate paper may be necessary. And this may not only concern data. Sometimes reports about internal processes facilitate inferences about methods of payment, applications etc.

7.4 PHYSICAL SECURITY

Besides the security problems directly connected to information and communication technology itself discussed further on there are the normal security aspects concerning buildings and equipment, which in most cases have to be solved physically.

7.4.1 Objects

These are some of security relevant objects:

- the whole area of a company or other organizations
- all buildings; and especially rooms that have direct communicative access to computer systems and communication installations
- utility services
- all hardware in conjunction with information and communication, mobile or fixed
- the adjacent neighborhood of the company grounds, inasmuch as access to internal systems may be attempted wirelessly.

All these installations have to be secured in different ways, once the potential for direct impact exists.

7.4.2 Access

The first and most important obstacle against non-authorized access is the selective accordance of admission to the installations of an organization. This subject will not be covered in detail here, since admission control is a science in its own right. It is important that always all currently available technologies be used to secure all rooms, which house central hardware for application systems by special admission mechanisms within or in addition to the already practised admission security to the premises themselves.

Terminal devices, which are placed in offices, should be physically fixed and switched off, when offices are deserted.

7.4.3 Threats

As will be outlined further down possible threats are manifold and specific for the area of wireless communications and surpass classical risk scenarios. They can be classified roughly in the following manner:

- direct access to central hardware with the intention to destroy or disrupt operations
- spying attempts on central applications
- spying attempts on decentralized applications
- attempts to manipulate central and/or decentralized data
- deployment of malware
- theft of terminal devices.

In addition there are other aspects to be followed up.

7.4.4 Equipment

Equipment commonly being subject to high risk potential are among others:

- central IT installations
- fixed peripheral devices
- mobile terminal devices
- external storage media
- communication modules (modems, ports, switches etc.)

7.4.5 Utility Services

Utility services are prone to create risks, once they

- do not function or
- function wrongly.

Electricity supply belongs to the first category. To prevent interruptions emergency power supplies have to be on standby. Water supplies belong to the latter category, if large quantities of water penetrate computer rooms and endanger hardware due to water pipe fracture. For both cases emergency plans have to be drawn up.

7.4.6 Disposal

Besides the usual legal disposal regulations special attention has to be drawn to additional aspects concerning company and IT security:

- Prior to disposal all data stored on devices – most important administration data – have to be deleted or neutralized in such a way that even accomplished technicians will not be able to re-constitute them.
- Indications to the company like type labels and inventory labels have to be removed. In this way inferences about the original company, where they were in use, should not be possible.

7.5 DOCUMENTATION

Here are the most important elements to be considered for individual directives:

- subject of the directive (hardware: laptop; software: intranet for example)
- application procedures for usage
- responsibilities for usage and costs
- limitations of usage and costs
- interdictions
- liability
- damages.

Directives are of a general nature or relevant to specific fields of technologies. One has to distinguish between the proper directive itself and the corresponding rules of implementation.

7.5.1 Processes

Quite similar to other aspects of IT quality management the Deming Process [100], so called after the famous American quality guru W. Edwards Deming, plays an important role for IT security philosophy with respect to verification, compliance and evolution. Figure 7.2 shows this process schematically.

Always the same cycle has to be passed:

system constitution > implementation > analysis > improvement

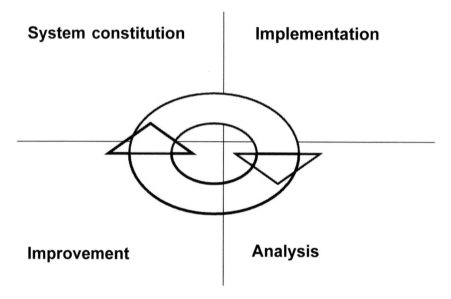

System constitution	Implementation
Improvement	Analysis

Fig. 7.2 The Deming Process

The policy outlined so far has to be prepared organizationally and technically. Thereafter implementation of it takes place together with all parties concerned. After a certain time of operation experience is gained resulting finally into new proposals and improvements. And the whole process starts all over again. It is important to note that the run time phase is not equal to a trial phase. In fact this is a continuing process with fixed review intervals. And its aim is not only to correct initial design mistakes. The overall process should rather make sure that especially within the IT environment the newest technological developments are taken into account regarding security aspects.

7.5.2 Commitment

A policy or directive without sanctionable commitment only possesses its paper worth, on which it is printed. Legally there are a number of possibilities to ensure the compliance with such a document.

7.5.2.1 Non-compliance

Notice to the IT security officer.

7.5.2.2 Acknowledgement of Instructions/Sample

This directive should be part of comprehensive employee security instructions. At the end the following agreement can be signed:

Acknowledgement of the Directive

"Please read the present … directive and countersign it at the bottom of the document. One copy with your signature will be kept by the IT security officer.

With your signature you acknowledge:

- I have received the … directive, understood its meaning and agree with it.
- confirmation of individual requirements from the directive
- confirmation of the confidentiality clause
- confirmation of liability and responsibility
- I understand that non-compliance regarding this directive can induce legal consequences.

  Name

  Signature

  Department

  Date"

7.6 WIRELESS SECURITY

Now elaborations from the preceding chapters can be brought in, for example:

- open and protected networks
- WLAN generations
- security requirements
- safeguarding availability
- securing data integrity

- securing authenticity
- securing confidentiality
- security risks
- PDAs
- general risk potentials
- strategic countermeasures
- technical countermeasures concerning IT security and communication
- distinctive risk potentials
- attacker holding a terminal device
- attacker not holding a terminal device
- Mobile Phones
- general risk potentials and strategic countermeasures
- general organizational countermeasures
- general technical countermeasures
- distinctive risk potentials concerning mobile phone communication
- attacker holding a terminal device
- attacker not holding a terminal device
- general protective measures
- Bluetooth
- instruments
- risk potentials
- countermeasures
- Infrared
- risk potentials
- countermeasures

7.7 SUMMARY

This general directive is the basis for other instructions and directives, which have to be worked out on a case-by-case basis for certain groups of people using certain technologies. Individuals concerned should be asked to commit themselves to those directives with regard to their fields of activity. The commitment takes place after instruction and training by signature of this separate document as outlined above. This present directive documents the strategic thoughts with respect to security of an organization, for which it has been drafted and as such is part of the overall IT or other security strategy and thus part of the company strategy as a whole.

References

[1] http://searchmobilecomputing.techtarget.com/definition/wireless-LAN

[2] IEEE Std 802.16-2009

[3] Code of Federal Regulations, Title 47, Volume 1, Revised as of October 1, 2001, Page 733-735: TELECOMMUNICATION,CHAPTER I: FEDERAL COMMUNICATIONS COMMISSION, PART 15–RADIO FREQUENCY DEVICES

[4] IEEE 802.11-1997: Wireless LAN Medium Access Control (MAC) and Physical Layer (PHY) Specifications

[5] IEEE 802.11: Wireless LAN Medium Access Control (MAC) and Physical Layer (PHY) Specifications. (2007 revision). IEEE-SA. 12 June 2007

[6] IEEE 802.11k-2008–Amendment 1: Radio Resource Measurement of Wireless LANs. IEEE-SA. 12 June 2008

[7] IEEE 802.11r-2008–Amendment 2: Fast Basic Service Set (BSS) Transition. IEEE-SA. 15 July 2008

[8] IEEE 802.11y-2008—Amendment 3: 3650–3700 MHz Operation in USA. IEEE-SA. 6 November 2008

[9] Hubert Zimmermann: "OSI Reference Model — The ISO Model of Architecture for Open Systems Interconnection", IEEE Transactions on Communications, vol. 28, no. 4, April 1980, pp. 425–432.

[10] Alhussein Abouzeid: "Wireless ad hoc and Sensor Networks MAC Layer Introduction & the IEEE802.11 standard", ECSE, RPI, September 15th, 2005

[11] IEEE 802.2-1998 (ISO/IEC 8802-2:1998), IEEE Standard for Information technology – Telecommunications and information exchange between systems – Local and metropolitan area networks – Specific requirements – Part 2: Logical Link Control

[12] Byeong Gi Lee, Sunghyun Choi: "Broadband wireless access and local networks: mobile WiMax and WiFi", Artech House, 2008

[13] Federal Standard 1037C

[14] Petar Popovski, Hiroyuki Yomo and Ramjee Prasad: "Strategies for Adaptive Frequency Hopping in the Unlicensed Bands", Aalborg University, IEEE Wireless Communications, December 2006

[15] Jan Boer: "Direct Sequence Spread Spectrum Physical Layer Specification IEEE 802.11", Lucent Technologies WCND Utrecht, 1996

[16]   S. Coleri, M. Ergen, A. Puri and A. Bahai: "Channel estimation techniques based on pilot arrangement in OFDM systems", IEEE Transactions on Broadcasting, Sep 2002

[17]   http://www.intel.com/products/centrino/

[18]   802.11i IEEE Standard for Information technology–Telecommunications and information exchange between systems–Local and metropolitan area networks–Specific requirements, Part 11: Wireless LAN Medium Access Control (MAC) and Physical Layer (PHY) specifications, Amendment 6: Medium Access Control (MAC), Security Enhancements, 2004

[19]   http://www.wi-fi.org/

[20]   Charles M. Kozierok: "The TCP/IP guide: a comprehensive, illustrated Internet protocols reference", No Starch Press, 2005

[21]   National Institute of Standards and Technology (NIST)
        ADVANCED ENCRYPTION STANDARD (AES), November 26, 2001

[22]   The Internet Society (2004), Network Working Group, RFC 3748, "Extensible Authentication Protocol (EAP)"

[23]   The Internet Society (2000), Network Working Group, RFC 2865, "Remote Authentication Dial In User Service (RADIUS)"

[24]   Pearson Studium, Andrew S. Tanenbaum: "Computernetzwerke", p. 268ff

[25]   "Specification of WAP Conformance Requirements". WAP Forum, WAP-221-CREQ-20010425-a

[26]   IEEE-Report: Status of Project IEEE 802.11n

[27]   IEEE P802.11 – Task Group p – MEETING UPDATE, Status of Project IEEE 802.11 Task Group p, 2010

[28]   D. Tse and P. Viswanath: "Fundamentals of Wireless Communication", Cambridge University Press, 2005.

[29]   Martin Johnsson: "HiperLAN/2 – The Broadband RadioTransmission Technology Operating in the 5 GHz Frequency Band", HiperLAN/2 Global Forum, 1999

[30]   Tamara Dean: "Network+ Guide to Networks", Third Edition, Course Technology, Bosten, Ma.

[31]   K. Fazel and S. Kaiser: "Multi-Carrier and Spread Spectrum Systems: From OFDM and MC-CDMA to LTE and WiMAX", 2nd Edition, John Wiley & Sons, 2008

[32]   Egevang, K. and P. Francis, "The IP Network Address Translator (NAT)," RFC 1631, May 1994

[33]   "Authorization of Spread Spectrum Systems Under Parts 15 and 90 of the FCC Rules and Regulations" (TXT). Federal Communications Commission. June 18, 1985. http://www.marcus-spectrum.com/documents/81413RO.txt

[34]   "IEEE Std 802.11-2007, Section 3.16, p. 6". 2007-06-12

[35]   How 802.11 Wireless Works: http://technet.microsoft.com/en-us/library/cc757419%28WS.10%29.aspx

[36]   F. Ohrtman and K. Roeder: Wi-Fi Handbook : Building 802.11b Wireless Networks, McGraw Hill 2003

[37] http://www.tech-faq.com/ssid.html

[38] Microsoft.com – Description of Internet Connection Sharing

[39] R. S. Roy and B. Ottersten: Spatial Division Multiple Access (SDMA), US Patent No. 5515378, 1996

[40] Pierangela Samartini and Sabrina De Capitani di Vimercati. Access Control: Policies, Models, and Mechanisms. In *Foundations of Security Analysis and Design: Tutorial Lectures*, Lecture Notes in Computer Science, vol. 2171, p. 137–193, 2001

[41] Wi-Foo: The Secrets of Wireless Hacking (2004) – ISBN 978-0321202178

[42] John Aycock: "Spyware and Adware (Advances in Information Security)", Springer, 2010

[43] "What is the Difference: Viruses, Worms, Trojans, and Bots?", http://www.cisco.com/web/about/security/intelligence/virus-worm-diffs.html

[44] Kevin J. Connolly (2003). Law of Internet Security and Privacy. Aspen Publishers, 2003, 131 pp.

[45] Lance Spitzner: "Honeypots tracking hackers", Addison Wesley, 2002 ISBN 0321108957.

[46] Rudolf Mäusl and Jürgen Göbel: *Analoge und digitale Modulationsverfahren*. 1. Auflage. Hüthig, 2002

[47] IEEE Std 802.11b-1999, §18.4.6.5

[48] B.P. Lathi: Modern Digital and Analog Communication Systems, Hault-Saunders, 1983

[49] Byeong Gi Lee and Sunghyun Choi: "Broadband wireless access and local networks: mobile WiMax and WiFi", Artech House, 2008

[50] Peterson, W.W. and Brown, D.T.: "Cyclic Codes for Error Detection". Proceedings of the IRE 49, January 1961, p. 228.

[51] Federal Standard 1037C

[52] 802.11i IEEE Standard for Information technology—Telecommunications and information exchange between systems–Local and metropolitan area networks–Specific requirements, Part 11: Wireless LAN Medium Access Control (MAC) and Physical Layer (PHY) specifications, Amendment 6: Medium Access Control (MAC), Security Enhancements, 2003

[53] Tanenbaum, Andrew S.: "Computernetwerken (Computer Networks)" (Fourth edition ed.). Pearson Prentice Hill, 2003

[54] David C. Plummer (1982-11). "RFC 826, An Ethernet Address Resolution Protocol – or – Converting Network Protocol Addresses to 48.bit Ethernet Address for Transmission on Ethernet Hardware". Internet Engineering Task Force, Network Working Group, 1982

[55] John Gantz and Jack B. Rochester: "Pirates of the Digital Millennium", FT Prentice Hall, Upper Saddle River, NJ, 2005

[56] "Wireless Networking Basics", NETGEAR, Inc. 4500 Great America Parkway Santa Clara, CA 95054 USA, 2005

[57] airsnort.shmoo.com

[58]   Matt Robshaw :"Fast Software Encryption: 13th International Workshop", FSE 2006, Graz, Austria, March 15-17, 2006, Revised Selected Papers (Lecture Notes in Computer Science), Springer, August 23, 2006

[59]   Tarek Sobh et al.: "Novel algorithms and techniques in telecommunications, automation and industrial electronics", Springer, 2008

[60]   "Wi-Fi Alliance Announces Standards-Based Security Solution to Replace WEP". *Wi-Fi Alliance*. 2002-10-31

[61]   IEEE Standard 802.1X-2004 – Port Based Network Access Control

[62]   "Extensible Authentication Protocol (EAP)", The Internet Society, Network Working Group, RFC 2865, 2004

[63]   www.openseaalliance.org

[64]   "US Allows Spectrum Use to Speed Up Wireless Communications", Computer, IEEE Computer Society, November 2010

[65]   S.J. Vaughan-Nichols: "Gigabit Wi-Fi Is on Its Way", Computer, IEEE Computer Society, November 2010

[66]   L.D. Paulson: "Wireless Devices Provide Users with Mobile Wi-Fi Hotspots", Computer, IEEE Computer Society, January 2011

[67]   AVM Computersysteme Vertriebs GmbH, Berlin, retrieved March 2011

[68]   "BlackBerry Pearl", *Research In MotionRIM*. 2006.

[69]   Viken, Alexander (April 10, 2009). "The History of Personal Digital Assistants 1980–2000". *Agile Mobility*

[70]   National Research Council (U.S.). Committee on the Future of the Global Positioning System; National Academy of Public Administration (1995). *The global positioning system: a shared national asset: recommendations for technical improvements and enhancements.* National Academies Press

[71]   Sweeny, Alastair (2009), *BlackBerry planet: the story of Research in Motion and the little device that took the world by storm*, John Wiley & Sons, Canada

[72]   BlackBerry Mobile Data System, http://us.blackberry.com/apps-software/mobile.jsp

[73]   Peter Machat Die Blackberry-Sicherheitsarchitektur aus der Nähe betrachtet", RIM, 2008

[74]   Bill Frank: "COMPACTFLASH® SPECIFICATION ALLOWS FOR THE ADDRESSING OF UP TO 137GB", CompactFlash Association Las Vegas NV, 2003

[75]   D. Geer: "Whatever Happened to Network-Access-Control Technology?", Computer, IEEE Computer Society, September 2010

[76]   Whitfield Diffie and Martin Hellman, "New Directions in Cryptography", IEEE Transactions on Information Theory, vol. IT-22, Nov. 1976, pp. 644–654

[77]   *Invention of the Year: The iPhone* (www.time.com am 31. October 31st, 2007)

[78]   3GPP TS 11.11:Specification of the Subscriber Identity Module – Mobile Equipment (SIM-ME) Interface

[79]   http://www.gsmworld.com/about-us/history.htm

[80]   ETSI EN 301 349 V8.4.1 (2000-10)

[81]   D. Collins, C. Smith: "3G Wireless Networks", MacGraw-Hill, 2001

[82]   M Haid: "HSCSD als Leistungsmerkmal im GSM-Mobilfunk der Generation 2+", Hagen, 2001

[83]   M Sauter: "Communication Systems for the Mobile Information Society", John Wiley, Chichester, 2006

[84]   GSM Doc 28/85 "Services and Facilities to be provided in the GSM System" rev2, June 1985

[85]   Wireless Application Protocol Architecture Specification WAP-210-WAPArch-20010712-a

[86]   J.R. Vacca: "I-Mode Crash Course", McGraw-Hill, 2001

[87]   J. Roth: "Mobile Computing". Grundlagen, Technik, Konzepte, Dpunkt, Heidelberg, 2005

[88]   http://www.umatechnology.org/overview/index.htm

[89]   RFC 3851: Secure/Multipurpose Internet Mail Extensions (S/MIME) Version 3.1 Message Specification

[90]   M. Hendry: Multi-application Smart Cards. Cambridge University Press, 2007

[91]   http://www.allaboutsymbian.com/features/item/Defining_the_Smartphone.php

[92]   "Voice over Internet Protocol. Definition and Overview". International Engineering Consortium. 2007

[93]   T. Rohwer et al.: "Abwehr von „Spam over Internet Telephony" (SPIT-AL), TNG, Kiel, 2006

[94]   http://www.bluetooth.com/Pages/Bluetooth-Home.aspx

[95]   J. Evans: "New Bluetooth Standard Approved", PCWorld, 2007

[96]   S. Rathi: "Bluetooth Protocol Architecture", Dedicated Systems Magazine, 2000

[97]   "Bluetooth Tutorial – Profiles"
       http://www.palowireless.com/infotooth/tutorial/profiles.asp

[98]   F. Bennett et al.: "Piconet Embedded Mobile Networking", The Olivetti and Oracle Research Laboratory, Cambridge, UK, retr. 2011

[99]   K. Scarfone and J. Padgette: "Guide to Bluetooth Security", National Institute of Standards and Technology, US Department of Commerce, Special Publication 800-121, 2008

[100] E. Uzun et al.: "Usability Analysis of Secure Pairing Methods", University of California, Irvine, retr.: 2011

[101] H. Bhatt and B. Glover: "RFID Essentials", O'Reilly Media, Inc., Sebastopol, California, USA. 2006

[102] T. Conneally: "Bluetooth 4.0 core specification released", 2010, http://www.betanews.com/article/Bluetooth-40-core-specification-released/1278425910

[103] Charles D. Knutson, Jeffrey M. Brown: IrDA Principles and Protocols. MCL Press, Salem UT 2004

[104] F. Deicke: "Optische drahtlose Datenübertragung", Fraunhofer IPMS, 2007

[105] M. Palmer: "Wireless Communication using the IrDA® Standard Protocol", Microchip Technology Incorporated, 2004

[106] K.W. Yeh and L. Wang: "An Introduction to the IrDA Standard and System Implementation", Hewlett & Packard, retr.: 2011

[107] ISO/IEC 13335-1:2004

[108] ISO/IEC 17799:2005

[109] ISO 17799 Newsletter: News & Updates for ISO 27001 and ISO17799, 2005

[110] R. Aguyao: Dr. Deming: The American Who Taught the Japanese About Quality, Fireside, 1991

Index